THE BIG PICTURE
Cinemas of Dundee

Author Jack Searle
with Craig Muir

Foreword by
Brian Cox

First published in the United Kingdom in 2012 by
Dundee Civic Trust

© 2012 Dundee Civic Trust

This book was written and produced by

Author Jack Searle with Craig Muir
Designed by Craig Muir

Publisher Dundee Civic Trust

ISBN 978-0-9548579-1-2

Printed in Dundee by PDQ

To find out about all our publications, please visit
www.dundeecivictrust. co.uk
There you can subscribe to our newsletter, browse or
download our current catalogue, and buy any titles
that are in print.

Contents

To Joyce

Foreward

When I was a young boy in Dundee, going to the pictures was a basic part of life. I just took cinemas and films for granted. What I did not realise at the time was that going to the pictures was far more popular in Scotland than in the rest of the United Kingdom, and that in Dundee it was more popular than anywhere else in Scotland. If I had been told at the time that there was one cinema seat in Dundee for every seven of its inhabitants, man, woman and child, I would just have thought that was normal.

What interested me was not that there were 26 cinemas in Dundee, but what was on at those cinemas. Films were exciting and gave a young boy thrilling visions of faraway places and cultures. I soon became as familiar with the Wild West, gangsters in Chicago, and night clubs in New York as I was with the Overgate in Dundee. But little did I realise at the time how things were going to change. By the time I was an adult not only the Overgate but all the cinemas I knew in my youth had vanished.

The fact is that the year of my birth coincided with the maximum number of cinema attendances in the UK. In that year 1.65 billion seats were sold in British cinemas. By the time I was ten that figure had declined by a third and was to carry on decreasing until 1986.

But since that low point cinema attendances have been slowly but steadily rising. It is highly unlikely that they will ever rise to the heights achieved in the 1950s, but there is now a healthy appetite for films. Ironically, although cinema going may be much less popular than in its boom years, today probably more people watch more films due to the heavy reliance by television on films as an essential and popular part of their programme schedules.

There is also a growing interest in the history of film as evidenced by the continuing flow of books on the subject and indeed television programmes and series dealing with the history of film.

Recently Dundee University Press published 'Jute No More', a comprehensive study of Dundee in the 20th century. One of its conclusions was that in Dundee, "the development of cinema was arguably the most important cultural phenomenon of the early twentieth century."

In the light of this it is good that the history of the development of cinemas in Dundee has been recorded and celebrated in this book.

Brian Cox
(Actor)

Introduction

Cinemas were places which had the power to transport people to fantasy worlds, to put them among mediaeval knights and in the depths of Sherwood Forest, to sail aboard a pirate ship, to live in an underworld where danger was always present and minutes later to be among the smart and sophisticated in a night club. In a cinema you could be thrilled and frightened, entertained and sometimes even made to cry.

As a child you could be a cowboy, a private eye, or a soldier, or even sail with Shirley Temple on the Good Ship Lollipop. As you grew up on the dance floor you were Fred Astaire or Ginger Rogers.

For most of us, films provided our only vision of ancient Rome or life at the court of Elizabeth. Going to the pictures was a way to see worlds that you could never visit in reality with the added comfort that the cinema was a place where the good guys always won.

Cinema buildings were a phenomenon of the 20th century and, as a building type, were one of the most transitory forms of architecture. They made an indelible mark upon the lives of the people of Dundee, and the story of cinemas and cinema going in Dundee is one that is well worthy of setting down. This book attempts to do just that.

Going to the cinema was more important in Scotland than in England. In 1939, the boom time for cinemas, the average annual attendance per person in England was 21, in Scotland it was 35. And cinema going was more important in Dundee than in any of the other cities of Scotland: in Glasgow there was one cinema for every 8,200 people, in Dundee there was a cinema for every 6,400 inhabitants.

It is difficult to be certain of the reasons for this but the over crowded housing, high rates of unemployment and low levels of wages were potent factors when an evening's warmth, excitement, and glamour could be had very cheaply at the cinema. Outwith the city centre, cinemas were community based which facilitated frequent visits to see films - even on a daily basis for some.

The idea for this book arose in 2010 when Dundee Civic Trust suggested the possibility of updating and revising the *Dundee Cinemas* book by Denis M. Naulty, which was published by the Trust in 2004. Following discussions with Denis, it was clear that he did not want his book to be changed as it was a personal reminiscence rather than a history of cinemas in Dundee. It was therefore decided to publish a separate history of cinemas and cinema going in the city. This book has built upon the sterling work done by Denis in producing his memoir. In particular the interviews that took place with some of those involved in the Dundee cinema business, who are sadly no longer with us.

This book does not pretend to be a history of cinema, but in order to give a proper context to what happened in Dundee, it has been necessary to give a brief outline of the development of moving pictures and major developments in the making of films.

The history of moving pictures in Dundee falls into four main periods. The first of these is the age of the Penny gaffs and of films as part of variety shows. this period runs from 1895 to 1910. The second started around 1910 when the Cinematograph Acts brought about a rush of new buildings designed specifically to show films, and lasted until the late 1920s when everything changed with the advent of the talkies.

The third period was the boom time for movies. It started in the late 1920s and lasted until the mid 1950s when television began to rob cinema of its mass audiences.

The fourth part runs from the mid 1950s until the present. The early part of this period saw a drastic decline in both cinema going and the number of cinemas operating in Dundee. The latter part saw a recovery in movie watching and the creation of the cinemas we have in the city as we travel through the second decade of the 21st century.

When carrying out the research for this book it soon became apparent that the experience of going to the pictures during each of these periods was quite different. Accordingly an account of what it was like to be a filmgoer at the time has been used to conclude the chapters dealing with each of the four periods.

No account of the story of film in Dundee would be complete without some attention being paid to the individuals who helped to create the buildings in which films were seen in Dundee, and the history of the buildings themselves. For this reason there are sections on the early pioneers of film in the city and the Movie Moguls of Dundee. The major part of the book gives details of what is known about each of the cinemas and other buildings where moving pictures were shown. The last chapter consists of brief accounts of the careers of some of those born in Dundee who made a career in pictures.

It was also felt that this book should not be just an account of film going in Dundee but also that it should set down the way that Dundonians felt about the cinemas to which they went. For this reason it was decided to include throughout a good number of quotes from movie goers in Dundee.

During the preparation of this book, it became clear that, in spite of extensive investigation and research, there may still be more information, particularly photographs, hidden away in the albums, cupboards and lofts of Dundonians and others. However personally treasured, if this material is not recorded in some permanent way, it is likely to be lost - either in house clearances, or by accident or decay. We would urge that all such material, particularly postcards and pictures, be made available in some form or another to bodies such as the Local History section of the City Library or at a national level, the National Library of Scotland or the British Film Institute.

After all, who would not want to contribute to their national heritage?

The Development of Moving Pictures

We now take moving pictures for granted as they are so accessible. Quite apart from the cinema we see them on television, our computers, and even on our phones. But it was not always so, and several inventions contributed to the showing of moving pictures to an audience. Indeed, something that we now take for granted only came about because of a series of developments that took place over centuries.

The first of these was the camera obscura - a darkened room or box with a small hole on one side through which light can enter and form an inverted image on a screen of the scene outside. It was first used by an Islamic scholar Alzahen (c 965-1039) to aid the observation of solar eclipses. In the 16th century, the introduction of a lens and a diaphragm improved the image obtained. By using a concave mirror, correction to the reversal of the image was then possible. The camera obscura could become a form of camera if light sensitive material was used so as to make a permanent record of the image.

The magic lantern was a development of the camera obscura invented in the late 17th century. Magic lanterns projected light through hand-painted or photographic glass slides which were inserted into the projector one at a time for small groups of spectators to view together. A skilled projectionist could move the slides quickly, making the images on the screen appear to move. With limelight, produced by a blowpipe flame directed against a block of quicklime, it was possible to project bigger images to a larger audience - but, as a result, the possibility of accidentally started fires drastically increased.

New sources of light (gas and eventually electricity) enabled projection to take place before ever larger audiences. Assisted by advances in photography, at the end of the 19th century, lantern showmanship had become a sophisticated audio-visual entertainment. Many of the shows had a musical accompaniment and often a narrator. Magic Lantern shows were certainly quite common in Dundee and were regularly put on by Peter Feathers later to become a pioneer filmmaker.

Probably the best known of magic lantern shows in Dundee were the touring shows put on by William Hamilton - firstly in the Kinnaird Hall and latterly in the Caird Hall. These were shown under the title of Hamilton's Diorama. This involved vast rolls of canvas which were wound onto vertical rollers on each side of the stage. There were painted pictures on the roll and two magic lanterns were used to project other pictures on to the canvas, one from the front and one from the back. By winding the canvas from one side of the stage to the other and manipulating the slides an illusion of movement was given.

Limelight illumination was superceded by the use of gas, and later electricity. The gas, William Hamilton remembers, "was in leather bags and as they became exhausted it was necessary for the projectionist to sit on the bag to keep up the pressure!". Although lanterns with three lenses could create dissolves and the illusion of movement they had now reached their limit. Nevertheless, the magic lantern had created a public taste for projected images that was the basis for the popularity of moving pictures in the years to come. Indeed, a whole year after moving pictures were first shown in Dundee a 'Grand Magic Lantern Exhibition' was held in the YWCA in Tay Street.

Poster for William Hamilton's touring show

William Friese-Green

When a pinpoint of light is moved rapidly in a circle in a darkened room, the eye sees the light as a continuous circle. This is due to a phenomena known as persistence of vision. During the 19th century, a number of attempts were made to exploit this to give the illusion of movement. Toys were developed such as the Thaumatrope, which relied upon a spinning disc and more importantly the Stroboscope which was the first device to produce illusion of moving pictures. Devices such as the Zoetrope and Reynaud's Praxinoscope developed these ideas.

Even with all of these developments, there were still problems to be resolved before moving pictures became possible. In order to take moving pictures photographs of moving objects must be taken at the rate of at least 16 frames per second. The first photos taken in the 1820s required an exposure of around eight hours to get even an imperfect image. Daguerre, a French artist, made advances which reduced the required exposure time to 10 minutes. Then, in England, Fox Talbot, by using silver salts, managed to reduce the period required down to one minute. In 1842, Daguerre got exposure time down to 15 seconds and, in the 1870s, R. L. Maddox brought it down to 1/25 of a second - a time that was sufficient to enable moving pictures to be taken.

Eadweard James Muybridge (1830-1904) in 1879, took a series of twenty four photographs using separate cameras which produced 24 frames of a moving picture. He mounted the pictures on a glass disc rotated in a device which he called the Zoopraxiscope to give the impression of movement. He toured Europe with this device where he met Professor E. J. Marey who further developed Muybridge's ideas. In 1888, Marey built what was the first successful moving picture camera, which took photos on a sensitised paper roll. However, his device was unable to take more than 40 pictures at a time meaning each roll ran for about a second.

The Lumière Brothers

Most negatives were still produced on glass and a strong and flexible film was required before any successful motion camera could be designed.

William Friese-Green (1855-1921), one of the best-known British film pioneers, had the idea of using thin strips of celluloid treated with chemicals to take the photographs. The celluloid had sprocket holes on each side of the film. He then developed a camera with a shutter which opened and closed several times a second, taking a succession of still photos. When the resultant film was projected rapidly onto a screen, this gave the impression of movement.

Thomas Alva Edison (1847-1931), was an American inventor par excellence (he held a world-record of 1,093 patents). He invented the phonograph, the carbon-button transmitter for the telephone speaker, the microphone, the incandescent lamp, a new generator of original intensity, the first commercial electric light and power system and an experimental electric railroad. Amongst this outpouring of creativity he also invented the essential elements of motion-picture apparatus.

William Kennedy
Laurie Dickson

However, he left the development of a practical camera for taking motion pictures to his employee, William Kennedy Laurie Dickson (1860-1935). Dickson, who claimed descent from Annie Laurie, had a Scottish father and a French mother. An early pioneer of cinema, Laurie led the work at Edison's West Orange laboratory. The results of Dickson's endeavours bore fruit in 1890 with the Kinetograph camera. This was a camera capable of taking pictures at a rate of 46 per second. In 1891 he developed the Kinetoscope peep-show viewer for watching moving pictures.

These were boxes that allowed images to be viewed by one person at a time by looking into it through a peephole.

The Edison Studios made many films most lasting about 20 seconds or so. Dickson was personally responsible for *Chinese Laundry* (1894), *The Irwin-Rice Kiss* (1896) and *Dickson Experimental Sound Film*. Then in 1885 George Eastman (1854-1932) invented the roll film of transparent celluloid strip 35 mm wide and coated with photographic emulsion. This enabled the laboratories of the Edison Company between 1886 and 1889 to develop a practical motion-picture camera.

Edison neglected to get foreign patents, considering the cost would be more than they were worth! Additionally Edison did not really like motion pictures and thought that their only real audiences were children, who would tire of them quickly. This was a decision that he would live to regret.

The viewing of moving pictures rapidly became popular and by 1894, The Kinetoscope Company (Norman Raff and Frank Gammon) began to set up Kinetoscope parlours, which rapidly spread across the United States. By the end of the year, ten of Edison's peep show viewers were imported and installed at 70 Oxford Street in London. The films shown were simple and basic unedited strips of footage.

Charles Urban (1867-1942) improved on Edison's work by inventing his Bioscope projector. He also produced the world's first successful natural colour motion picture system, Kinemacolor. Bioscope (a view of life) became a popular word and for a long time was the general name for the cinema, especially on British fairgrounds. From 1897 Urban worked in London from where he took and exhibited propaganda films during the First World War and did much to establish the documentary, news, travel and educational film.

Travelling Bioscope Show

Le Cinématographe Lumière: projector

Bioscopes, with their ornate show fronts, were features of travelling fairs at the turn of the 20th century. Some of these could be quite elaborate. George Green, a showman based in Glasgow, toured Scotland and Northern England between 1911 and 1914 with his Theatre Unique. This was a massive piece of equipment with a huge organ which opened out to form a large stage accessed by two staircases. (It is interesting to note that some 30 years later, Green's two sons built **Green's Playhouse**, probably the best cinema, - and certainly the biggest, ever to operate in Dundee). It is likely that machines like this were part of travelling shows that were put on at the Greenmarket in Dundee.

The race to produce a practical projector for moving pictures now involved a considerable number of people of different nationalities. A number of film projectors were developed by, among others, Skladonowsky, LeRoy, and Eugene Casler and had been the subject of public demonstrations before December 1895. However, it is widely recognised that it was the Lumière brothers, Louis (1864-1948) and Auguste (1862-1954), from Lyon in France, who gave the first successful public showing of projected pictures thrown onto a large screen.

Their father, Antoine Lumière, had bought an Edison Kinetoscope in 1894. The Lumières worked to overcome the limitations of the Kinetoscope. They patented the resulting combined camera and projector in February 1895, calling their invention the 'Cinématographe'. This was the first successful projector, which also took film.

The Lumière's short films were shown to a paying public for the first time on the 28th December 1895, in the basement of the Salon Indien of the Grand Café at 14 Boulevard Des Capuchins in Paris. The Lumières showed twelve films. These included 'Watering the Gardener', which was probably the first comedy film and an early 'documentary', *Workers leaving the Lumière Factory*. Thirty-three spectators paid a franc each to see the wonders of moving pictures.

Clearly the genie was now out of the bottle and things would never be the same again.

Kinetoscope Parlour

Moving Pictures – the early days (1895-1910)

2

After 1895 films developed very rapidly, the principal countries involved being France, the United States and Britain.

France

Moving pictures really came of age at the Paris Exhibition of 1900. Films were shown by the Lumière Brothers on a giant screen, 25 metres by 13 metres. Some films were shown with a recorded dialogue. Also shown were widescreen pictures filmed on a 75mm film as opposed to the 35mm format that was then (and later), the norm. Coloured films were also screened, although it was not until 1907 that the Lumières launched their 'Autochrome Lumière' process onto the market.

Prominent among the pioneers in France were George Melies, Pathé Frères and Leon Gaumont. Melies set up the Star Film Company in 1896 and over the next ten years made over 500 films. He was the genius of the early film-making period and took on the roles of producer, designer, director, writer, cameraman and actor. He covered a great range of subjects including fantasies, docudramas and historical dramas. He was also the first film maker to treat film as artistic medium. However in 1911 his career was over when he sold out to Pathé Frères who, with Leon Gaumont, had virtually ruined him by plagiarising his films.

Pathé Frères was established by brothers Charles, Emile, Theophile and Jacques Pathé and by 1911 had become the major film company in France. They not only produced films in their own country but also distributed and exhibited them throughout the world. Pathé had acquired the Lumière Brothers patents in 1902. This was the essential element which allowed them to design an improved studio camera and then to produce their own films. Pathé soon dominated the international market. They first moved into London where they set up a chain of cinemas before expanding across Europe, America, Australia and Japan.

Their only real competitor in Europe was the Gaumont Film Company been founded by Leon Gaumont in 1895. The company was extremely successful and in 1905 Gaumont created what were then the largest film studios in the world. However these were soon to be surpassed in America where the nascent film industry was growing with phenomenal speed.

United States

A number of people were now developing their own projectors and cameras. William Dickson with others had formed the American Mutuscope Company in December 1895. This later became the American Mutuscope and Biograph Company and provided significant competition for Edison who went down a different path by manufacturing other's inventions under the Edison name.

In September 1896 Thomas J. Armat and Charles F. Jenkins demonstrated (in Atlanta) a motion picture projector called the Phantoscope. This was eventually manufactured and marketed by the Edison Manufacturing Company who renamed it the Vitascope. Following its first showing at a music hall in New York the Vitascope soon became a common feature in vaudeville and variety theatre shows across the USA. In Britain the Vitascope was known as the Vitagraph and in 1898 on the 8th January the **Gilfillan Hall** was showing 'The Vitagraph with new scenes and Animated Photographs'.

In 1902, the opening took place of the first permanent cinema in the USA. This was The Electric Palace in Los Angeles. In the same year Edwin S Porter, who had started in films as a projectionist for Edison, made *The Life of an American Fireman* (1903). This film incorporated documentary footage and showed a story from both from the viewpoint of a fireman and of the young woman who he was rescuing.

United Kingdom

As in France, there were a number of pioneers working in the early days of film. The first documented showing of moving pictures in England took place on 14th January 1896 at the Royal Photographic Society and was presented by Birt Acres. A month later the first public film show of moving pictures in Britain took place on the 20th February 1896 in the Polytechnic Hall in Regent Street, London. The show was presented by Monsieur Towey, a friend of the Lumière brothers, using their hand-cranked Cinematograph machine which they had developed only one year previously. In March 1896, in Olympia in London, Robert Paul gave a screening to a paying audience using the Theatrograph projector that he had developed himself.

In Scotland, the first public display of Edison's Kinetoscope peep show machines took place in Edinburgh on Christmas Eve 1894, at H. E. Moss's Christmas Carnival in the Waverley Market. In Dundee, in the following year later, there was a showing of Kinetoscope machines in a shop in the Overgate (probably No. 40).

The first recorded public screening of movies in Scotland to a paying audience was on the 13th April 1896 at the Empire Palace Theatre in Nicholson Street, Edinburgh, with a showing of Edison's Kinetoscope loops on a cinematograph projector. The first public showing in Scotland of the renowned Lumière machine took place in Glasgow on the 16th May 1896 at the Ice Skating Palace in Sauchiehall Street, where a show was presented by Arthur Hubner.

It was in Scotland that films were first given the seal of respectability when on 3rd October 1896, Queen Victoria and her guests (including Tsar Nicholas II of Russia), were filmed at Balmoral by J & F Downey of South Shields. These were probably the first films ever taken of British Royalty.

Another London enthusiast, David Devant, toured the northeast of Scotland with a show in the autumn of the same year, as did R. W. Paul with his Theatrograph, or Animatograph, as it was sometimes known.

The First Films in Dundee

On the 8th July 1896, the **People's Palace** in the Nethergate advertised in the Dundee Courier :

> *'Grand Re- opening Monday August 9th*
> *Mr. Sheldon has engaged at Enormous Expense*
> *PAUL'S ANIMATOGRAPH*
> *Direct from the Empire London*
> *To give a GRAPHIC and complete illustration of the*
> *Queen's Jubilee Procession'''*

The Courier reported on 10th August that "Paul's Animatograph pictures formed one of the principal attractions of the evening". This is the first record of moving pictures having being shown in Dundee.

Two months later, on 7th October 1896, Mr Peter Feathers advertised in The Courier his first public showing of movies in Castle Street where he had hired a room in the **Royal British Hotel.** On 8th January 1897 the **Kinnaird Hall** was showing *Animated Pictures* as part of a performance of Hamilton's Diorama.

By now Queen Victoria seemed quite happy to engage with the idea of being filmed and gave permission to William Walker of Aberdeen to film her at Balmoral on 22nd May 1897. Later that year, in October, Walker presented a programme of films at Balmoral which included scenes from her Diamond Jubilee procession in London. Walker, one of the early Scottish filmmakers went on to establish a Scottish tradition for making documentaries and was to later visit Dundee to give screenings on a number of occasions.

During 1897, films began to be shown in Dundee on a regular basis. On 3rd September 1897, the **Kinnaird Hall** again advertised moving pictures, this time being shown by Walker & Company. On 15th October a film show took place in the **Gilfillan Hall,** and in November Peter Feathers gave a show of *Special Local Scenes and Humorous Pictures* in the large Hall at the **YMCA** in Constitution Street.

Although there are no documented records relating to Dundee it is likely that from 1897 moving pictures were featured in travelling shows such as those toured in Scotland by the Green Brothers, Mackney and J. Wingate. At this time it was also common for moving picture shows to take place in empty shops, in temporary booths or in the penny gaffs in which theatrical shows were given.

While the first films shown were just scenes that ran for about sixty seconds each, it soon became possible to make longer lengths of film. Later, by gluing together several of these, it was possible to make up even longer films of up to ten to thirty minutes. These were shown in canvas booths, shops, circuses, sideshows and halls.

A travelling show featuring moving pictures

One such venue was the **Booth in William Street,** run by Robert Pennycook. He recalled that, "Performances lasted only about an hour but people flocked to see the jerky, blurred images that appeared on the screen three times a night". Another booth established in Dundee at around this time was located in Bellfield Street, owned by Arthur Henderson.

It was not surprising that, given the limitations of early films and the often down market locations in which they were shown, films were regarded by many as a passing and limited fad for the first ten years of their existence. Nevertheless despite the doubts, the popularity of films continued to grow.

From around the end of the nineteenth century techniques improved dramatically. Many innovations were made in England, notably by Robert Paul, who not only manufactured his own version of the Lumière camera, but also invented the camera dolly which allowed tracking shots. A contemporary of Paul was George Albert Smith who was the first to film action sequences and then project them in reverse. In 1898 he was the first to mount a camera on the front of a railway train and film a journey- a shot much used by early filmmakers - including Dundee's Peter Feathers. In 1900, Smith also put the first close-up on film.

In these early years, programmes just showed scenes that ran for about a minute each which was all the 65 to 80 feet standard length of films could produce. The subjects of these shorts were simple scenes of real life or stage acts. One cinema goer recalled going to the cinema when one the films was entitled "The 10.30 Express. This consisted of a scene showing passengers boarding a train, the guard waving a flag and the train pulling out". Bill Illingworth, who spent his life working in the cinema industry, recalled that "A picture of 1,000 feet called for special billing at that time". He also recalled a colour sequence in a film that showed the hero with a blood red face.

Colour

The showing of coloured films was more common than is usually thought, as there was a desire to have colour films from the very inception of moving pictures. The principle of colour photography had been discovered by Scot James Maxwell in 1861. Early and simple methods of applying colour to film by tinting or toning, (usually by hand), were in use as early as 1900. But the first instance known of coloured pictures being shown in Dundee was on 3rd January 1903, at the **Forester's Hall** when 'living pictures in lifelike colours' were shown. This was a programme of short films.

Although the first colour stencilling system for moving pictures had been launched by Pathé in 1905, the first commercial colour process was introduced in 1906 when the Kinemacolor 2 colour additive system was patented by G. W. Smith and combined with Urban's Kinemacolor projector. The Kinemacolor projector exposed alternate frames through red and green filters mounted on a wheel in front of the camera. When developed and printed, the resulting black and white film was projected through a similar filter wheel mounted on the front of the projector. Urban's Kinemacolor projector unfortunately was plagued by difficulties which included rapid wear and tear of the film and colour drift from one part of the frame to another. In addition the somewhat complicated apparatus needed to show the films was less than ideal and thus never caught on.

Without a proper colour film system the first method of applying colour was by hand tinting or toning. This was used widely during the era of silent films and employed by such luminaries as D. W .Griffiths and Melies. The first full length colour film was a hand tinted effort – *Ali Baba* (1905) by Pathé. In 1909, *Psyche* a full length coloured film, was shown in the **Gilfillan Hall**. From the way the advertisements for films specifically drew attention to the fact that they were coloured it is likely that coloured films were quite unusual at this time.

Films progress

Gradually a more sophisticated cinema industry grew up to replace the early brief films that were fill-ins between variety or circus acts or diversions for the audience at travelling shows. The length and scope of the films developed rapidly as did the numbers of cinema shows. This was assisted by the greater availability of projection equipment. Theatres began to buy their own Lumière derived projectors many of which were given names to intimate the exclusiveness of the venue. Hence the **King's Theatre** in Dundee gave shows on its 'Kingoscope' while the **People's Palace** showed films on its 'Paloscope'.

The Great Train Robbery

Between 1900 and 1903, *chase* films developed where characters were pursued, creating an atmospher of speed and excitement.

Edwin S Porter introduced the *story* film when he released his *The Great Train Robbery* in the USA on the 15th June 1903. This was an 8 minute film showing a gang of bandits taking over a train and being pursued by a sheriff's posse. It had gunfights, chases, and armed hold-ups and set a pattern for the first Western films. The climax came when a bandit fired a pistol pointed at the audience. This was excitement of a kind peculiar to film. It set the pattern for continuity editing and for the westerns that became so popular in both the silent and sound eras.

As films developed, so also did the industry that produced and distributed them. In September 1902 the French film pioneer Georges Melies invented the genre of film science fiction with the release of his 14 minute film *A Trip to the Moon*. By the 3rd January 1903 this film was being shown to audiences at the **Kinnaird Hall** in Dundee, an example of the speed and effectiveness of the distribution system that had already grown up for this nascent industry.

In 1903 the **Gaiety Theatre** became a venue for the screening of moving pictures when on the 30th June it gave a showing of films by Royal Canadian Animated Pictures that included a film of *Life in Canada* which ran to 10,000 feet.

By 1905 moving pictures were shown in a number of locations in Dundee. On the 4th December of that year the **Empire** advertised 3 performances a day of:

> *Prince Edward Century Animated Picture Co.*
> *40 MILES OF THRILLING AND FUNNY PICTURES NIGHTLY*
> *Greatest Cinematograph in the British Isles*

George Méliès 'Le Voyage dans la Lune' (A Voyage to the Moon)

Just one week later the **Gilfillan Hall** held a show given by NEW CENTURY ANIMATED PICTURES. A flavour of what was presented was given in the 12th December edition of the Evening Telegraph & Post which reported that:-

"Last night a large and very appreciative audience in the **Gilfillan Hall** welcomed to Dundee a visit of the New Century Animated Pictures. These pictures – the finest in their line - form a complete entertainment in themselves and an entertainment in which the interest never flags. At one time the audience shriek with laughter at

The Adventures of Mr Jones. The next moment the audience are moved to pathos and excitement by pictures such as *The Sailor's Wooing*, where the newly married husband is rescued just in time from a burning ship, and *Rescued by Rover* where the sagacity of a dog rescues a stolen child. It shows the alert up to dateness of New Century Pictures that scenes are shown from films which have just arrived in this country of the Prince and Princess of Wale's tour in India".

The True Story of the Kelly Gang

Although *Rescued by Rover* was a pioneering film recently released by Cecil Hepworth, and famed for its narrative form, most of the films shown at the **Gilfillan** that night were quite short with little plot development. But shortly afterwards, in 1906, the first feature length film *The True Story of the Kelly Gang*, was produced by John Tait in Australia. This had a film length of 4,000 feet and lasted for an hour.

News films had already gone beyond this. At the **Gaiety Theatre** in Dundee, a showing of film of a boxing match in 1906 lasted for one hour thirty minutes in total, although there may well have been gaps between the rounds. News reels were very popular at this time, particularly when they featured scenes of war. Films of the Boer war at the turn of the century attracted large audiences. This was not altogether surprising when the only visual alternative was the sketches and drawings found in the newspapers of the time. However the future of the cinema lay with feature films, not newsreels.

Reels of film became longer. By 1908, 'nickelodeon' shows in America were lasting one hour and admission cost 10 cents. The shows were made up of several one reel films - a reel of film was 300 metres or 1,000 feet and ran for about 10 to 15 minutes. These became very popular. The great popularity of films had its drawbacks however, as the content drew the attention of government who were always concerned at what the populace was getting up to. In 1908, to give an element of control over this new and rapidly growing medium, the American Board of Censors was set up.

In 1910, the first motion picture was filmed in Hollywood. Running for 17 minutes, it was entitled *In Old California*. In the same year the first filmed version of *Frankenstein* was directed by J. Searle Dawley for the Edison Kinema Company.

In November 1910, a report in the Courier and Advertiser noted that, "The moving picture has taken a fair hold of the Dundee population. The photographs are touched up, so to speak, with a running commentary by several humorists behind the screen which adds greatly to the audiences' enjoyment. The titles of some of the attractions – *The Victims of Fate*, *The Angel of the Dawsons Claim* serve to indicate the melodramatic nature of the fare that was served up".

Time for Change

As the length of films grew, so did their range of subjects and versatility which led to new and bigger audiences. Such was the popularity of moving pictures that they were screened in virtually any kind of structure. But longer films brought their own hazards and the chief of these was fire. This brought about major changes in the development of cinemas and cinema going.

Fire was a factor that had been present, even in the days of the magic lantern displays that were so popular around the turn of the century. In February 1905, Dundee's firemen were called out to deal with a fire in Lochee Road that had been caused by the overturning of a magic lantern.

But celluloid films were altogether more dangerous. In 1897, one hundred and fifty people died in a fire in a Paris cinema caused by a projector that had burst into flames. Fires sometimes occurred in kinetoscopes and, as films got longer, cinema fires became commonplace. The frequency of fires in cinema shows was, perhaps only to be expected given the flammable nature of the nitrate film used and its closeness to a very hot lens that only became hotter as the length of films increased. There were disastrous outbreaks of fire in cinemas during the earlier years. Closer to home, there were a number of fires in some of the penny gaffs in Dundee.

Not surprisingly this became a matter of concern to the City Council. As early as the 14th March 1906 the Firemaster reported to the Police Committee on "the danger of Cinematograph Entertainment in the City". He reported that "At present in nearly all the places where such entertainments are held, the operating apparatus is exposed and in the event of anything taking fire, the audience would be in great danger. I would therefore recommend that at such places where we have power, the operating apparatus should be worked from a fire-proof box of sufficient size and that a responsible person is placed in charge of the lights". The Committee agreed and instructed the Firemaster to go ahead.

In all this Dundee was a pioneer in taking firm and specific action to prevent fire. At the national level, the Cinematograph Act (which was designed to deal with this problem) was not passed until 1909 and even then the Act did not become effective until 1910. However this did make it compulsory to have a separate projection room, adequate exits and proper fire precautions.

But implementing Dundee's pioneering action was not without its problems. In January 1908 the Police Committee considered the matter of attendance and cost of providing firemen at shows. This remained an on-going concern. On 20th December 1912, members of the Police and Lighting Committees of the City Council met to confer with licensees Messrs Spink, Griffan, Noble, Feathers, Lunn and Howard on the subject of the provision of firemen during cinema entertainments. And as late as May 1913, Arthur Henderson was arguing against the level of fire precautions required at his moveable booth in Anderson's Lane in Lochee before he could be granted a licence. However the Committee was unrelenting and Henderson backed down.

The 1909 Cinematograph Act also brought about a proper system of licensing and the universal requirement for fireproof projection rooms. Similar concerns brought in similar regulations all around Europe and America but sad to say they did not eliminate the unhappy connection between cinemas and fire.

In Limerick in Ireland 50 people died in September 1926 and 69 were killed in a cinema fire in Paisley in December 1929. In Dundee fires continued to occur in cinemas including, among others, the **Tivoli**, the **New Cinema** (twice), the **Casino Picture House** and the **People's Palace**.

While a few purpose-built cinemas had been built before 1910, the coming into operation of the 1909 Act meant that the age of the fairground cinema shows, the cheap and popular 'Penny Gaffs' and the unregulated showing of films as part of theatrical shows, had to come to an end.

Going to the gaffs - sitting in the stalls.
While most early cinema had various devices to attract customers, for most people it was actually the sensation of being in the cinema that evoked most memories. But the experience of cinema going changed radically throughout the years.

In the early days there were basically two ways to see moving pictures. The first of these, and the most basic, was the Penny Gaff or showman's booth. The second was to see them as part of an evening's entertainment in a theatre or variety show.

Attending a film show in a booth, such as those run in **Blackness Quarry,** in **Bellfield Street** by Arthur Henderson and by Joe Noble in **Anderson's Lane** in Lochee, was a fairly basic experience but could be an exciting affair in more ways than one. Weather was a constant hazard and occasionally booths were blown down - as occurred at Arthur Henderson's Booth in **Bellfield Street**.

On entering the booth one would probably pass animated musical figures used to drum up custom and a chocolate boy selling sweets. Sometimes there was no seating and patrons stood on earthen floors, but often temporary seating was the rule. This was provided on planks balanced on whatever supports came to hand. Children would attempt to get in under the temporary canvas walls.

Breakdowns were frequent and, as Robert Pennycook observed, "The audiences gladly suffered the discomfort of sitting on wooden planks, but they would not accept the frequent breakdowns. Objects were thrown at the screen. The pianist doing his best to entertain the audience was drowned out by the thunder of stamping feet."

The accommodation afforded by travelling shows was often far more substantial than that provided by the booths. In travelling shows in the early days, one might queue to see Peep Shows provided by rows of kinematograph machines or, after the turn of the century, to sit on benches to see a variety programme that included some short films.

In the town many people saw moving pictures for the first time in the Overgate in a shop that charged for seeing Peep Shows on the new Kinematograph machines. A much more comfortable experience would have been to attend one of Peter Feathers' shows which he held in a room at the **Royal British Hotel** in the High Street. In February 1901, in unlikely surroundings of the **Gilfillan Hall,** football supporters could look forward to a screening which included "Holiday Football Match - Hibs v Dundee, weather permitting Mr. Feathers will take special scenes". This was probably first showing of a Dundee football match. Films of local football matches proved popular. In March 1903 the **Peoples Palace** put on a show advertised as:

> Animated Pictures - Scenes from the Dundee Cup tie
> Great Fights with the Hibs.
> 20,000 lifelike portraits of the Spectators.

For many, particularly the middle class, their first experience of moving pictures would have been as part of a variety show at the **People's Palace** or the **Gaiety Theatre**. the films shown in theatres were often short newsreels or films of current events. On the 2nd April 1909 a variety show at **The King's Theatre** included a newsreel show on what the theatre called 'the Kingoscope'. Comedies were specially popular and in these shows an audible audience response to on screen events was the norm, including cheering, hissing or booing.

The Silent Screen (1910 -1927)

3

The result of the City Council's decision in 1906 to require proper fire precautions in cinemas, and the passing of the 1909 Cinematograph Act, was to eliminate the penny gaffs and to reduce the supply of cinema seats just at the time when demand for moving pictures was rapidly expanding. Dundee entrepreneurs reacted swiftly and a veritable flood of building activity took place.

1910 saw the opening of the **New Cinema** in Morgan Street, **Edwards Picture Palace** in Bonnybank Road, the **Electric Theatre** in the Nethergate, and the **Edenbank** in Watson Street. The following year the **Britannia** opened in Smalls Wynd, the **People's Picture Palace** in Logie Street, the **City Picturedrome** in Milnfield Road, and **Nobles Picture Palace** in Andersons Lane, Lochee. 1912 saw the opening of the **Main Street Picture Palace**, the **Magnet Picture Palace** in Well Road, the **Star Electric Theatre** in Balgay Street, Lochee, the **West End Cinema** in Shepherds Loan and the **Hippodrome** in the Hawkhill.

During the period leading up to the First World War developments across the Atlantic took place that would influence film making throughout the world. One of these was the development of film stars, famous in their own right.

It was only in the period after 1910 that notion of film stars first really took hold. This was because most early films were of real scenes and news events. However as dramas and comedies became more prevalent the early movie makers felt that, as in the theatre and music hall, popular actors would demand more money, a feeling that proved more accurate than they ever anticipated. As a result they did not credit actors on their films. This lasted until 1910 when Florence Lawrence became the first star credited on film. By 1912 she was earning $80,000 per annum.

After this the dam broke and stars such as Pola Negri, Clara Bow, Theda Bara, Louise Brooks, and the heroine of many cliff-hanger serials, Pearl White, became famous all around the world. Male stars such as Rudolph Valentino, Ramon Navarro, and William S. Hart also emerged. One of the most popular western star to emerge at this time was William Duncan from Dundee. Surprisingly, even animals such as the canine hero, Rin Tin Tin, became popular, and villains calculated to chill the blood, such as Bela Lugosi, had their own fan clubs. In 1914 the most famous of all the stars, Charlie Chaplin, debuted in his first feature film.

The studios quickly realised that the promotion of stars equalled the promotion of the films they were in and of the studios that made those films.

Even in 1913, with the shadow of armed conflict looming in Europe, the openings took place of the **Pavilion** in Alexander Street, the short-lived **Uno Picturedrome** in Lawrence Street, Broughty Ferry, and the magnificent **La Scala** in the Murraygate. **La Scala** quickly identified itself as a cinema for the middle class. Its first two screenings were *Moths*, a screen adaptation of a novel by fashionable English author Ouida (1839-1908) and *Psyche*, the first Kinematograph version of the mythological legend. In 1914, on the eve of hostilities Arthur Henderson opened the **Queens Cinema** in Bellfield Street.

These openings of new establishments were in addition to a significant number of upgradings of the theatres and locations where films were already being shown.

Censorship

Dundee was not alone in having a cinema boom and the increase in cinema going brought to a head what had been an ongoing matter of concern for some. This

Bela Lugosi

was the belief that the showing of films in the dark encouraged immorality in the cinemas. When it was determined that the terms of the Cinematograph Act of 1910 would enable local authorities to censor film content, the film industry was so worried that they decided to set up their own body to deal with censorship. This was the British Board of Film Censors, set up in 1912 to enable self regulation by the film industry. This dealt more with what was happening on the screen rather what might happen in the cinemas'.

The BBFC soon issued guidance on what kinds of things should be deleted from films. At the top of the list was 'Scenes holding up the King's uniform to contempt or ridicule', 'Subjects dealing with premeditated seduction of girls', 'Unnecessary exhibition of under-clothing', 'Men and women in bed together', 'The irreverent treatment of sacred subjects', and lastly, 'indecorous dancing'. The original cause of the concern - immorality among the audiences - was left to the efforts of torch wielding usherettes to detect untoward activity and eject those concerned.

The attitudes behind these rules were still being felt in 1927 when the French film *The Passion of Joan of Arc*, regarded as a classic all around the world, was banned in Britain because of its portrayal of English soldiers. In February 1930 no less a person than George Bernard Shaw derided the film censors for banning *The Night Patrol* - a cinematic portrayal of night life on the Thames Embankment - because it actually showed prostitutes on the screen.

The First World War

The onset of the First World War came at a time when there was a major change underway in the kind of films being screened. Up to then cinemas generally gave short programmes of single reel films. But by December 1915 Peter Feathers' **Electric Theatre** in the Nethergate, whose early shows were all about local events, was advertising not newsreels but dramas.

> 'Houses of Terror 3 Reel
> Ashes of Happiness 2 reels
> Pathé Colours'

This kind of show was even then being replaced by a programme that consisted of a major feature of four reels or more with a supporting programme of films which might include a cartoon and a newsreel. The **Victoria Palace Theatre** showed a 5 reel film, *The Beggar Girls Wedding* and in the same month **The Kinnaird Hall** advertised the Italian classic silent film *Cabiria*. This was a major epic with a cast of thousands - a 14 reel film lasting around three hours.

Cabiria 1914

However the First World War had serious repercussions for cinemas and the film industry in Britain. After an initial lack of understanding of what films could do for propaganda, the potential of the greatly increased demand for news from the front was soon understood by all the governments of the warring nations. Official films were taken of action on the Western and Middle Eastern fronts such as *The Battle of the Somme* (1916), and of the war at sea. These were very popular just as, initially, were the 'Roll of Honour' pictures of soldiers serving at the front. However, as the fatalities increased the latter fell from favour, whilst the films related to military action always guaranteed a good audience. On 2nd January 1915 the **Kinnaird Hall** advertised the following programme:

> 'Kinomacolour War Picture'
> 'With Fighting Forces in Europe'
> Programme includes:-
> Belgium Loyal and Brave, Germany-Know Thy Enemy
> Serbia – The Scapegoat of the War
> Great Britain and her Empire – Mobilisation of Kitchener's Army
> "Sons of Empire" etc France - Steadfast Friend
> Japan – Our Ally in the East, Turkey – The Sick Man of Europe
> Russia – The Colossus of the East

Films encouraging women to support the war effort on the home front were also part of filmgoers' wartime fare. An example was *The Life of a WAAC*, a recruitment film for the Women's Army Auxiliary Corps made in 1918. Those going to the **Gilfillan Hall** could have seen *The Kaiser's Spies*.

One area of growth in European film making, stimulated by the war, was the making of newsreels. In 1897 Charles Pathé, a Frenchman, had introduced short motion pictures of current events in England. Newsreels were then shown regularly, first in music halls between entertainment acts and later between the feature films in moving-picture theatres. Newsreels covered current events such as parades, sports contests and news of disasters, such as floods and fires.

The war also needed to be funded and one of the tax measures introduced by the government in 1916 was an Entertainment Tax. This was a flat rate tax and had a heavy impact on the price of the cheaper cinema seats – a 2½d ticket became 4½d - a rise of 80%. There were many protests about the tax which was reduced in 1920, but not abolished.

The onset of the First World War also meant that during the period of hostilities the supply of films from European makers was drastically diminished. Most of the demand was therefore satisfied by the United States where the growth in demand for movies had led to film making on an industrial scale.

The output from Hollywood increased rapidly, and the formerly dominant industries in France and Italy were overwhelmed as American films powered into the world market. To cope with the demand major film studios were already being established in America. Before the war had even started, in 1912, Universal Pictures had been set up and the pace quickened as hostilities got under way - Fox Film Corporation was established in 1915, along with the Metro Picture Corporation in the same year. In 1916, the Goldwyn Picture Corporation was started, whilst 1917 saw Louis B Mayer Pictures established.

The result was that the British market was flooded with American films. It has been estimated that in 1914 about 45% of the films shown in the UK were British. The rate of decline of the British film industry can be seen from the fact that by 1926 the British share of their own market had fallen to just 5%.

The outbreak of the First World War not only had a great effect upon the film making industry in Europe, it also had significant implications for cinemas in the UK. In 1914, there were about 4,500 cinemas in operation in the UK but changes in the structure of the industry meant that almost a quarter of these had closed by the end of hostilities.

However, the war years did not see a complete cessation of cinema building in Dundee. The **Royal** in Arthurstone Terrace was up graded in 1916 and the **Broughty Ferry Picture House** was opened in the same year.

The war even had an aftermath for the showing of films in Dundee. In Scotland virtually everything was shut on Sunday but in 1918, the City Council agreed to 'a series of kinematograph exhibitions' to be held on Sundays at the Caird Hall for the Postmen's War Memorial Fund'.

The greater length of films now possible allowed for more complicated story lines and this opened up the possibility of adaptations of novels, plays, and even opera. By 1910 it has been estimated that one third of films were based on plays and a further quarter on novels. This in turn made cinema attractive to a larger and better off audience, leading to the creation of larger, more luxurious buildings in which more sophisticated films could be shown.

An example was the showing in April 1919 at **Her Majesty's Theatre** of *Hearts of the World* and the advert is worth quoting in full to see the market at which some films were aimed.

D.W. GRIFFITH'S
Picture Marvel

HEARTS OF THE WORLD

Cinematograph art makes a notable stride in such a production as
Hearts of the World. To witness it is at once an education and an entertainment.
The Mightiest, Most Astounding Photo Play. Exactly as shown at the Palace
Theatre, London, and by Royal Command Performance to H.M. the King and
Queen at Windsor Castle.

Far better than The Birth of a Nation and Intolerance.

Note. Hearts of the World will never be presented at any but the Highest Class
Theatres at prices charged for the Best Theatrical Attractions - D W Griffiths

---

Nevertheless by the 1920s the American film industry was totally dominant. This could clearly be seen in Dundee. Films such as the *The Sheik* with its star Rudolph Valentino generated long queues. In 1924 the success of *Robin Hood* with Douglas Fairbanks at **The Kinnaird** was such that the film was shown for a second week, and for the first time in Dundee - continuous performances were shown throughout the day.

In total contrast, in March 1924 the City Council sponsored the showing in most Dundee cinemas of a film entitled *An Enemy within our Gates*. It was described as being "very interesting without being very pleasant" which was not altogether surprising as it was part of the City Council's Rat Week campaign.

American comedies were particularly popular especially those with stars such as Charlie Chaplin, Buster Keaton and Harold Lloyd. Chaplin's nostalgia and sympathy for the underdog might have been sentimental but it was incredibly popular with cinema audiences. Ironically the avarice of the film industry exploited this very popularity. In 1928 film distributors refused to allow cinemas to book Charlie Chaplin films unless they took a package of less popular films. This lead to a boycott of Charlie Chaplin films in Dundee. The cinema owner's stand ultimately proved unsuccessful due to the boycott breaking activities of **Shand's Picture Palace**, which carried on booking Chaplin's pictures on the distributor's terms and attracted so many customers that they had to extend opening times.

In the same year, the 1,600 seater **Plaza** on the Hilltown was opened by Lord Provost Phin - a mark of how important cinemas had become in Dundee. This was reinforced by the conversion of the **King's Theatre** to the 1,400 seat **King's Theatre Cinema**.

Charlie Chaplin - The Kid

Douglas Fairbanks
The THIEF *of* BAGDAD
'HE WILL STEAL YOUR HEART AWAY!'

In spite of the great popularity of moving pictures, earlier developments held on for a while and the Diorama was still a regular Christmas entertainment in the early 1920s. In the face of cinema newsreels it had given up on the portrayal of news events and tended to show only travelogues supported by variety acts. Even then it had to have moving pictures as part of the programme. This can be clearly seen from the review in the Courier of a presentation in the **Caird Hall**.

"The Programme for 1924-25 Season invited the audience to travel round the world in 120 minutes by means of colossal scenery, wonderful transformations, and absolutely the finest scenic paintings'. The 27-scene world tour began at London's Piccadilly Circus ('the centre of the world') and ended by arrival in the River Mersey. In between, patrons had seen Cabaret in Paris, an earthquake at Lisbon, a bullfight in Spain, the peace of the Chapel of the Nativity in Bethlehem, a Turkish Café in Constantinople, the moonlight in Mauritius, the capture of an Arab slave dhow in the Red Sea… An orchestra played and there were topical and comedy pictures projected by 'an up-to-date Kinematograph Mechanism' at Intervals".

But moving pictures were moving ahead on all fronts. Pathécolour had been around for some time, and Kinemacolour had been seen in Dundee as early as1915. Technicolor arrived in 1922 although it was not really perfected and available for general use until 1932. In 1927, a widescreen film process was developed by Warner Brothers with their Vitascope system. Specially composed and recorded music accompanied the better films.

Acting techniques had been developed to cater for everything from slapstick to sophisticated comedy, from romantic dramas to biblical epics, from westerns to tales of Gothic horror. And it was not just the acting that had improved.

By the end of the 1920s, silent films had developed into a highly sophisticated form. In the upper class **La Scala** in 1929 the Evening Telegraph gave a film the kind of review that easily have could have been found in the Courier's reporting of plays in the theatre.

"The first independent film Anthony Asquith has produced is shown at **La Scala**. Mr Asquith has taken the everyday aspect of London's underground and has transformed it into a setting of romance. From its crowds he has drawn a group of wonderfully human characters and in presenting their story has achieved an imaginative work of remarkable brilliance. On 'Underground' he is to be heartily congratulated. It is a production that cannot fail to enhance the value of British-made pictures in the estimation of cinemagoers. The story is simple but it has not an atom of staleness about it. Love and jealousy in humble life is depicted and the sensational climax - one unique probably in film history - is conveyed so convincingly that a strong sympathy between audience and player never falters. Even the tremendous tragedy at the end, while it horrifies, does not destroy the tie between the spectator and the villain. In him an excellent character study is included. Too human to be thoroughly despicable, he is one of the four principals, each of whom is human enough to have a share of good and bad points. Brian Aherne, Elissa Landi, Cyril McLaglen and Nora Baring skilfully use the dramatic material".

But many of the skills so painfully learned by the silent stars were to be thrown out of the window with the coming of talkies.

Watching the Silent stars

The first thing that the cinema-goer would notice in the age of silent films that there was no lack of sound in the auditorium. Firstly, there was the sound of the audience. Not only would there be contributions from audience members who were used to participating in music hall performances, but also there would be the mumbling of those who could read, explaining the subtitles that were projected onto the screen to their friends, who either could not read or who were poorly sighted.

To enhance the experience, dialogue was often supplied by speakers standing behind the screen. Given that the speakers were always locals and spoke in the local dialect, this gave another dimension to the action, particularly when a scene was set in a Royal Court in Italy or in a temple in ancient Rome, and the dialogue was in broad Dundonian.

Sound effects were also commonly supplied, often by the use of halved coconut shells to simulate the noise of horses' hooves, or by slapping pieces of wood together to simulate a gunshot. There was even a device to provide the sound of rainfall. On some occasions nature took over when the sound of rain on the tin roof of the cinema blotted out everything else. Words of popular songs of the day were shown on the screen and mass singing of them took place.

Nearly all cinema showings had the benefit of a live musical accompaniment. This could vary from a lone piano to a full orchestra, according to the size of the cinema. Music was used to express the mood of the film and punctuate the action. According to Mr Bill Ramsay, one time manager of the **Astoria** and the **Victoria**, "the speed of silent films was often adjusted to suit the timing of the accompanying music".

In Dundee, talented local musicians formed orchestras in most of the large cinemas. The largest was the 18 piece orchestra on **The Scala** led by Harry Hollingworth who also played in **The King's**. In the smaller cinemas audiences could be more unruly. Stories are told about pianists being barraged by orange peel and other objects necessitating the erection of protective glass screens or wire netting to fend off the rain of missiles.

James Hinchliffe was well known for playing accompaniments to the silent films shown in the **Caird Hall**. On one occasion, he played from over 300 pages of special music to fit every mood of a 2¼ hour picture. The show opened at Christmas and was so popular that at New Year, Mr Hinchliffe was required to perform at 4 showings of 2¼ hours each - a marathon feat of playing.

Hinchliffe also played the organ in the **Caird Hall** in later years. Other Dundee cinemas offered organ music. **The Forest Park** had a small pipe organ for a short time until the coming of the talkies. The **Cinerama** had a harmonium, as did the **Palladium**.

Dundee had two other cinema organs, both of the church type. One was in the **Plaza**, Hilltown. It was a 3-manual with 864 speaking pipes giving it about 14 manual stops plus probably a couple on the pedals. It lasted only a year or so in the cinema – by 1929 it was in a church. The other was in the **Kinnaird Picture House**, Bank Streer. This former civic hall had a good example of a mid-Victorian concert organ dating from 1864. The firm of Forster & Andrews, Hull, had installed it at a cost of £1,300. This organ continued to be played when the hall became a cinema. It was a very fine comprehensive instrument of 4 manuals and 48 speaking stops.

The availability of musicians led to a mixture of stage acts, films and music that persisted in the **King's** right up to the advent of sound. A programme staged in July 1929 was reported thus. "Patrons of the **King's Theatre** will this week enjoy a first-rate programme. The principal film, *Hell Ship Bronson*, is a strong tale of the sea. Highly melodramatic, it is a gripping story, full of tense situations. The supporting picture, *Obey Your Husband*, is a dramatic story of modern marriage. On the stage is an exceedingly clever and original turn by the Plattier Brothers. With their acrobatic musical interlude and clever bird imitations they add greatly to the enjoyment of the programme. Orchestral selections of Scottish melodies, an organ solo by Stephen Robinson and the P.C.T. (Pictorial Complete the Attractions)".

Dundee now had a good range of cinemas but these varied widely in quality. The ranking was emphasised by the journals in which they chose to advertise. All the cinemas operating in Dundee advertised in the Evening Telegraph but only the **King's**, the **Kinnaird,** the **Gaiety**, and the **People's Palace** advertised in the Dundee Courier.

A colloquial term for some of the poorer cinemas was "the fleapit". This was the case in most cities and was not altogether surprising given that at this time a great number of households had no baths or indeed inside lavatories. Many families only resort for basic hygiene was to go to the public baths. As a result many picture houses were sprayed with disinfectants, particularly during the children's matinees. Even when things got better the many owners preferred to use perfumed sprays throughout the auditorium to give a better ambience. The best example of this was the 1936 advertisement for the opening of **Green's Playhouse**. Among the lists of suppliers of everything from steelwork to seats, could be found an advert for the supply of perfumed sprays to the new cinema.

Green's Playhouse - Interior

The Dundee Pioneers

4

In Dundee the first public screening of moving pictures was at the **People's Palace** in the Nethergate in July 1896. However, the next screening of moving pictures was given on 6th October 1896 by Peter Feathers, the film-making pioneer of cinema in Dundee. Feathers (1858-1943) was born in Broughty Ferry to a father who was an optician and chronometer maker.

Peter Feathers

Peter was educated at Dundee High School, after which he was trained as an optician by his father. From early on he had an interest in the rapidly developing field of photography. It was, therefore, no surprise when he started his own business at 6 Castle Street. From the very start he operated not only as an optician, but also as a photographic dealer and photographic apparatus maker.

His interest also encompassed the projection of pictures as can be seen by his 1893 advertisement when he advertised in the Dundee Courier & Argus 'For sale or hire, Magic Lanterns and Lantern Slides. Catalogues on application. Peter Feathers, 6 Castle Street'. He was also a regular advertiser in the short lived journal 'The Piper o' Dundee.

On 7th October 1896, he became the first Dundonian to give a public screening of moving pictures in Dundee. Feathers later explained the way in which this came about. He was visited in his shop by the representative of a French firm, (almost certainly Lumière), who offered him a cinematograph machine and a few films. Although his only previous experience was with Magic Lantern exhibitions he bought the machine and some films. He subsequently gave private views to a number of his friends. Feathers then engaged a room in the **Royal British Hotel** and put the following advertisement in the Courier of 7th October 1896:

> "The Latest Novelty
> Animated Photography
> Exhibitions Given Daily at 12, 3, 6, 7 & 8"

This was the second public screening of moving pictures in Dundee. In the very same month he gave a screening at the High School Bazaar which proved to be extremely popular.

However he soon became interested in making his own films and went on to become the city's first film-maker. On 6th November 1897 the Courier advertised a screening of his films in the Large Hall of the **YMCA**, Constitution Street as follows:

> Peter Feathers
> GRAND EXHIBITION OF MOVING PHOTOGRAPHS
> By Mr Peter Feathers

Initially the films he made were of local events and scenes. For example, he filmed workers leaving Baxter's Mill and notably the inspection of the First Forfarshire Volunteers in Baxter Park. He also showed great enterprise in 1897 getting the agreement and active cooperation of the North British Railway Company to make a film of the rail journey from Tayport to Dundee. He managed to get the Company to provide a special engine with a fish truck in front which gave him a wonderful view as the train crossed the River Tay. Feathers photographed the entire rail journey

Peter Feathers

from the truck. This included shots of railway workmen and was one of the first movies of this nature in Scotland to be made.

Feathers soon began to expand his range of subjects. He was a great traveller and always took his movie camera with him. He went on a boat to St Petersburg, visited the Greek Islands, and travelled across central Europe. This provided material for the films that he made himself. By 4th February 1901, Feathers' shows had graduated to the more upmarket venue of the **Kinnaird Hall** where he presented 'Animated Pictures' on his 'new electrical projector'. The bill was also more upmarket and consisted of:

> 'Historical Living Pictures'
> Victoria driving through Windsor on her 80th birthday
> Our New King and Queen
> Diamond Jubilee Procession
> The Funeral procession in Dundee showing clearly all the Dundee notables

The last of these was almost certainly made by Feathers himself and was designed to bring the customers in.

By the time of Feathers last but one show in his 1901 season at the **Kinnaird Hall** he seemed to be short of customers if the advert below is anything to go by:

> 'Feathers Celebrated Animated Pictures'
> "The Biggest, The Brightest, The Best, The Novelist collection of animated pictures ever exhibited
> Free handsome three guinea hand camera for selecting the 10 most popular pictures.
> Somebody will get this camera - why not you'"
> "NB. Please bring a pencil".

For the last show in the season Feathers gave what was probably the first showing of a programme of films especially screened with children in mind. This was advertised as:

> Special afternoon performances for the young folks on Saturday at 3pm.
> The first 1,000 visitors entering the hall will each receive an artistic Souvenir.
> Admission 2d, adults 6d.

Feathers showed his pictures when and where he could. As time went on he found a growing demand for his film shows, especially in the rural areas, and engaged and trained several assistants to help him with his presentations. In the winter of 1903, Peter Feathers went north with his team of helpers to exhibit his cinematographic pictures in the Trades Hall, Aberdeen. In 1904, Feathers showed his 'Feathers Cinematograph' machine in the same location. This seems to have been an apparatus that he had developed himself but there is no information on how or when he developed the machine.

However, although Feathers continued to show his films in a number of venues in Dundee, such as the **Gilfillan Hall** and the **Kinnaird Hall**, he saw a need for a permanent base. He therefore acquired a 'portable' theatre in William Street, which consisted of four collapsible wooden walls and canvas roof. This was his first **Electric Theatre**. In it he showed programmes of short, simple films. Normally he gave three performances each night 7-8pm, 8-9pm, and 9-10 pm. Like many of the penny gaffs it was pretty basic. Seats were provided by means of wooden planks

EXHIBITIONS
OF
Animated
Photographs
GIVEN AT
Concerts, Festivals, &c

CHOICE SELECTION
OF
OPERA GLASSES,
TELESCOPES, FOLDERS,
AND
SPECTACLES.

PETER FEATHERS,
OPTICIAN,
6 CASTLE STREET, DUNDEE.
From the 'Piper o'Dundee

balanced on metal drums. Underfoot was an ash and sawdust covered earthen floor. Around 1908 he sold the William Street booth to Robert Pennycook for £60.

Feathers opened his second **Electric Theatre** in 1910 at 122 Nethergate. This was located in an adapted shop which stood where the Marketgait now runs. A typical programme at this time was made up of news films and other short films of events that he would buy in, such as the *Royal Visit to Dublin*, the *Investiture of the Prince of Wales*, and *Elephant Racing at Perak*.

Now that Feathers had his own permanent premises he could put on full programmes of his own films. These tended to be local in nature such as the Scots Greys passing through Dundee to Barry Camp, people on the High Street, a passenger train leaving Dundee East Station and local Highland Games. There were continuous showings from 2.30 until 10.30pm and an orchestra gave an accompaniment to the films. But Feathers' mind was on greater things and in 1911 he sold the business.

This was because in 1910 he had commissioned the building of a new cinema that could also take on variety shows. This opened in 1911 in Morgan Street and was named **The New Cinema**. It had 850 seats and a small balcony to the side of the screen to accommodate an orchestra.

He used the cinema to give showings of his own films. A typical show took place May 1914 when The Courier advertised that at the New Cinema there would be a:

'Grand Galaxy of local films.
Dundee Territorials' Church Parade in Victoria Park.
Boys' Brigade Inspection in Baxter Park. Masonic Church Parade.
The above films specially taken by Mr Peter Feathers.'

In the same year Feathers changed the name of his Morgan Street premises to reflect the fact that cine-variety shows were also on offer. Thus the **New Cinema** became the **Stobswell Cinema-Theatre** under which name he operated the building until he sold it on in 1929.

Films were not just a business for Feathers but an obsession. He operated cinemas throughout a 30 year period in which films moved from silent flickering images shown in fairgrounds, to talkies shown in purpose built cinemas.

Even after he retired he remained active on the local scene. He was still an active member of the Dundee & East of Scotland Photographic Association when, at the age of 84, he died on 18th May 1943. An enthusiast for films for all of his life, he was truly a pioneer of film showing and film making in Dundee.

A plaque commemorating his great contribution as a pioneer film maker was placed on the wall near his old shop in October 1996. Donated by 'Cinema 100' this was part of a national scheme to mark special events in Britain's cinematic Centenary. This was an overdue public recognition by Dundee of its pioneer film-maker.

Arthur Johnson Cook Henderson

A softly spoken man, Arthur Henderson came from a fairground family and performed in London music halls as an acrobat. He first came to Dundee in 1896. The family toured in caravans drawn by traction engines that also provided power for the shows. Eventually Arthur settled in Dundee and by 1899 he had premises at Anderson's Lane, Lochee. These served as his base and winter quarters for his travelling show. The premises were also used to stage drama performances and to screen short films.

Henderson also showed short silent films in the 1890s in a canvas booth in a quarry in Bellfield Street. This was located where the St Joseph's Primary School later stood. Here he showed motion pictures in a fairly primitive wooden framed tent.

In February 1946, he recalled, "I charged a penny a time, gave three shows nightly, often entertaining between two and three thousand a night. On other nights the audience was smaller, and on one night takings reached the large sum of three shillings and sixpence. One night especially will always live in my memory. A sudden gust of wind - the worst enemy of the old pavilion - blew the whole show down on top of the audience.

Arthur Henderson

I was manipulating the apparatus from the little box at the rear and from that position could see nothing of what was happening when the cross beams of the roof came clattering down. Nothing was left standing except the front of the show, but no one was hurt and people scrambled out as best they could". Many people came round to the front, asking for their money back and when Henderson counted out the evenings drawings he found himself seven shillings and sixpence out of pocket.

McIndoe's Show

By 1906, Arthur also ran an early cinema show in a basic building on ground between Nelson and Wellington Streets. Six years later Henderson built the **Wellington Palace** on the site. Henderson also used the trade name of McIndoe - and many people called it 'McIndoe's Show'. He remained the owner of the **Wellington Palace** until it was burned down in 1930.

Henderson continued to tour together with his brother-in-law Hugh McIndoe and in Aberdeen in 1897, showed a short programme of silent films. Later, in 1910 Henderson applied to build a cinema in Aberdeen. His proposal to erect a large corrugated iron shed with wooden benches and without toilets, was turned down by Aberdeen Council. A further application with the addition of toilets was also rejected. Henderson then turned his attention back to Dundee where up to 1913, he continued to put on temporary shows in the Greenmarket over Christmas and New Year.

In 1911, he established **The Britannia Picture House** in Small's Wynd and ran it until 1936 when he sold it on to J B Milne.

In 1914, Henderson built the **Queen's Cinema** on the site of his former booth in Bellfield Street. This he operated until 1928 when it closed following the opening of Henderson's new **Alhambra** cinema on the other side of Bellfield Street.

After the 1914-18 War, Mr Henderson acquired an old rectory in Well Road and subsequent to its conversion opened it in 1922 as **The Queen's Hall Cinema**. Eleven years later his love for drama resulted in a change of direction. In 1933 he renamed it the **Queen's Theatre** and ran six seasons of repertory productions. However these were not as successful as was necessary and it reverted to a cinema in 1939.

The Alhambra / State
Bellfield Street

Alhambra Picture House. It opened in 1929 with seating for 1,039 people and was designed by Frank Thomson the son of the famed city architect and engineer. It was originally constructed as a cinema but with the possibility of theatre performances. For a period between 1937 and 1939, Henderson did actually hold live theatre shows in the **Alhambra**.

Henderson had a son, also Arthur (1893 - 1962) who, with his father, ran the **Wellington**, in Wellington Street, the **Britannia** in Small's Wynd and the **Alhambra**. Around 1930 he left Dundee and went on the music halls for a number of years. He later returned to Dundee where he worked as chief projectionist in the **State Cinema**, Bellfield Street. The Alhambra was sold by Henderson in 1941 to the Pennycook family

Arthur senior was a great enthusiast for early silent films and had a stock of these, one of which was *Daddy Long Legs* which starred Mary Pickford. When he met Mary Pickford at a lunch at the Gleneagles Hotel she told him that it was the one of her films of which she had no copy. Arthur promptly mailed it to her.

Arthur Henderson senior died in Dundee on 15th May 1953. A pioneer of cinema in Dundee he was always torn between his enthusiasm for film and his love of theatre. Perhaps it was a fitting memorial to him that his **Alhambra** cinema, renamed as the **Whitehall Theatre,** eventually became the principal venue for amateur dramatic groups.

Daddy Long Legs

Joseph Bell

Joe Bell was born in 1879 in Dundee. According to the obituary in the Courier he was a colourful character, being in his time a gambler, bookie, philanthropist, showman, entertainer, actor, dance hall owner and songwriter. He started his working life as a part-time employee in a jute mill but added to his meagre earnings by carrying on a betting business on the side. As off - course betting was illegal at the time, this was a somewhat risky activity. Nevertheless around 1910 he started the first football pool in Dundee. This pioneer pools promoter switched to entertainment in 1912. Otherwise, it might have been 'Bell's' instead of Littlewoods Pools that went national.

At one time he was involved with a cinema in South Road, Lochee called **The Casino Picture Hall**, a corrugated sheeting structure. The name of the cinema probably reflected his activities as a betting man.

Joe Bell

The Broadway
Arthurstone Terrace

The price of every seat was a penny and a full house of 1,000 people made the total taking £4 4s!. The Casino has a varied life, being run as a cinema for silent films, theatre/music hall, roller skating rink and as a dance hall. It burned down in 1929. Always generous, during a long strike in Lochee in the 1920s, Joe bought 2,000 loaves of bread and 12 tons of potatoes that he distributed to the needy people of Lochee from the Casino.

In 1912, Bell bought **The Grand Theatre** at 22 King Street, Broughty Ferry. This was a basic building with a corrugated iron roof which was very noisy in heavy rain. This tended to drown out the musical accompaniment to the silent action on the screen. The basic seating consisted of long wooden benches in the front rows costing 2d. Joe sold it in 1918 for £1,800.

Bell's next move was to buy **The Picture House** (1918-31) in Arthurstone Terrace. Here he put on films and variety shows, presenting the famous Scots comedians Harry Gordon and Will Fyffe amongst many other artistes. It later became **The Royal Picture House** (1931-61).

In 1928, at 39 Erskine Street, Joe built another tin-roofed theatre with straight wooden benches and named it **The Empress Playhouse**. He sold it for £2,500 in 1932 to Mrs Shand who renamed it as the **Broadway Theatre**.

As his last project Joe had plans to build in Hilltown, on ground just south of Ann Street, but he sold the site for £1,800 to Mr Headrick, a local businessman who built **The Plaza**.

Joe Bell was reputed to be the greatest gambler in Scotland. He certainly was at times a wealthy man but went through his fortune, probably because of his predilection for gambling. Although in his time he was quite wealthy, in old age he lived almost entirely on the state pension and died in 1964.

Arthur Edward Binnall

Arthur Binnall came from Rochdale in Yorkshire. A small dumpy man he always wore a morning suit when on duty. His first venture into cinemas was his conversion of St Mary's Church Hall in Well Road which he operated as a cinema until 1911/12.

Around 1911, he had become sufficiently prosperous to contemplate building an entirely new cinema. This was one of the first purpose built cinemas in Dundee - the **Hippodrome.** This was located at the corner of Well Road and Hawkhill as was opened in 1912. In 1917, he sold the **Hippodrome** to the Macintosh family who modernised the entrance and renamed it the Princess.

In 1922, he took over the **New Empire Theatre** in Rosebank Street. This was the cinema that later put on the first double bill programme in Dundee. This was made up of two feature films, a Mack Sennett comedy and a 10 minute newsreel. Binnall sold **The Empire** in 1927 to Singleton.

Binnall also renovated the **Casino** in South Road. Binnall seemed to favour Lochee as the location for his cinemas. In 1927, he built the **Rialto** in Gray Street, bought and modernised the **Astoria** in Logie Street and renovated the **Casino Picture Hall** in South Road.

In late 1936, he sold his cinema interests to the Grays and moved back to England. Arthur Binnall may have finished his life in Lancashire, but he left a reminder of his time in Dundee as he named his house 'Rochdale'. The name can still be seen above its door in Ancrum Drive next to the Albert Hall.

5 The Talkies - Sound and Success (1928-1953)

Sound had been provided to accompany films from as early as 1903 when Gaumont provided recorded musical accompaniment for significant numbers of their films. But it was not until 1910 that sound systems had sufficient amplification to be used in a full size cinema.

Even then the introduction of sound to motion pictures was not a simple matter. In the USA, over 1,000 films with a sound track were made between 1923 and 1927 using the Phonofilm system but these were all made for specific reasons - often the recording of political speeches or musical performances at the opera for example.

There was also a widespread distrust of the idea of sound among the film studios themselves who were worried at the difficulty and expense of equipping vast numbers of cinemas around the world with sound systems. They were also well aware that changing subtitles on silent films was a much cheaper and simpler way of making them suitable for all countries around the globe, compared to filming in different languages or dubbing the films.

Films with sound tracks looked like a much more difficult proposition. To make matters worse, initially there were many different sound systems, all with totally new technology in need of improvement.

Another problem was the addition of music. Until 1933, music could not be added after the film was made. This meant that in the early days an orchestra had to perform on the set of the film as the filming went on, with all the attendant problems that this entailed.

It took Warner Brothers to break the log jam by making *The Jazz Singer* in 1927 and *The Singing Fool* in 1928. These films turned out to be a great success, not because they were talkies, but because of Jolson's off-the-cuff dialogue, which seemed spontaneous and real when set alongside the declamatory dialogues previously shown on film. The financial success of these pictures led to a mad rush by the other studios to join Warners in the bonanza. The result was a flood of talking pictures, particularly musicals. This was not altogether surprising as the musical was the one film genre which could not be supplied by silent films.

In 1928 Warner Brothers released *Lights of New York* which was the first all talking feature film. It was made for $23,000 and took over $1,000,000 at the box office. The success of talkies was assured.

In Britain the first studio to start making talkies was the British International Picture Company who inserted a short talking sequence in its 1928 picture *Kitty*. Other studios quickly followed suit and the implications for the UK film industry quickly became apparent. Make talkies or die!

In Dundee the introduction of talkies had a complicated and somewhat chequered start. The owner of the **Royalty Kinema**, William Pennycook recalled that at that time talkie technology was imperfect to say the least. "A number of the early talkies employed sound discs rather like vast gramophone records. These were quite separate from the films. If all went well it was fine, but if there was a break in the film the sound discs went on until stopped. When the break was repaired it was almost impossible to synchronise the image with the sound on the record".

The advent of the talkies led to a significant increase in movie attendances which in turn led to the building of many new cinemas. In 1928 Dundee saw the opening of the **Rialto** in Lochee, the **Plaza** on the Hilltop, and the **Forest Park Cinema**. In

Caird Hall
One of two valve amplifiers

the following year the opening took place of the **Alhambra** and the reconstructed **Astoria**. There were also many alterations undertaken on existing cinemas, the owners deciding not only to install equipment to project the new talking pictures, but also to carry out an upgrading of the whole cinema. There were numerous examples of this in Dundee, such as the **Kinnaird** and the **Broadway. Her Majesty's Picture Theatre** underwent major internal redesign and re-emerged as the **Majestic Cinema** in 1930.

The first talkie programmes had a somewhat reserved reception from the local media. On 9th July 1929, the Evening Telegraph reported as follows:

"'All Talkie' Programme at the **Kinnaird** crowded audiences yesterday witnessed the presentation at the **Kinnaird Picture House** of Dundee's first 'all talkie' and 'sound' programme. The feature film obtained by the management for this big event is *The Cohens and the Kellys in Atlantic City*. It is in a way a pity this film is first on the list of 'talkie' attractions at the **Kinnaird** for, though the sound synchronisation is perfect, the dialogue is difficult to follow. This is not due so much to any mechanical defect as to the very pronounced American accent of all the characters and which the British ear finds difficult to follow. In spite of this, however, the film was well received and when we remember the fact that this invention is only in its infancy we cannot but feel that there is a great future for it".

Nevertheless, *The Cohens and the Kellys in Atlantic City* was not popular due to the thick New York accents identified by the reviewer, and the **Kinnaird** lost money on it.

The gaucheness of some early talkies when both actors and directors were coming to grips with sound quickly passed. New techniques of filming combined with improvements in cameras and microphones soon produced a much more sophisticated product. Above all, sound allowed for the first time the production of musicals. These became immensely popular and *The Broadway Melody* was the first real talkie success for the Kinnaird.

The use of films with integrated sound tracks eventually cured this problem but the frequency of breakdowns in early films was a major drawback.

In Dundee the changeover to talkies took some time and **La Scala** did not show its first talkie until 1930. Initially it was only the two reel films that were talkies – main features remained silent as did many short comedies. The May 1930 newsletter given by Arthur Binnall to his patrons and set out below gives a flavour of the scene at that time:

The outstanding event for this month is *Innocents of Paris* starring Maurice Chevalier who has been acclaimed the new Valentino. In this talking picture he sings numerous songs in English and French which are bound to please all who hear them Another outstanding picture at The Rialto is *The Girl from Havana*, starring Lola Lane, the wonderful singer from *Movietone Follies* fame.

The Godless Girl is the big attraction for the Astoria this month. This is a Cecil B DeMille super production dealing with the awful conditions prevailing in the big American reformatories. Incidentally this is the last of the big silent productions which you will see in Dundee.

We have a real treat for the women folks on 8th May when we are showing *The Mad Hour* at the Astoria. This is a daring story of married life by the wonderful writer, Elinor Glyn."

The Mighty Wurlitzer organ

One of the consequences of sound was the unemployment of most of the musicians who accompanied silent films in Dundee. Cinema orchestra players asking for more money were an additional cause - sometimes they cost more than the hire of the films shown! Some orchestras were kept on for a while to play during the intervals and between 'houses'. However the increasing availability of organs designed for use in the cinema led to some cinema proprietors installing theatre organs in their auditoriums when orchestras became too expensive to maintain. Two of the organs used in Dundee were models known as the Mighty Wurlitzer. These could provide the sound effects of trumpets, tubas, clarinets, oboes, xylophones and drums. So impressive were these giant organs that the instruments became attractions in themselves.

By 1930 cinema-going had become an established part of the cultural scene in Dundee. New cinemas continued to appear in the city – the **Vogue** in Strathmartine Road, (1936), **Green's Playhouse** (1936) and the **Regal** in Lochee in 1937. Cinemas were rapidly growing both in number and quality, and many buildings originally designed to put on theatre performances were altered or re-equipped. Examples of this were the **Majestic** in the Seagate, the **Plaza** in the Hilltown, the **Royal** in Arthurstone Terrace, and the **Victoria** in Victoria Road. Even the **Caird Hall**, surely Dundee's most prestigious concert venue, put on regular cinema shows on Saturdays and Sundays.

Another mark of the popularity of films was that in 1934 George Kinnear founded the Dundee & St Andrews Film Society which by 1948 had over 1,100 members and a waiting list of 100. The aim of the Society he said, was "to give a series of performances of films of the highest artistic merit". This it proceeded to do giving showings of the *Battleship Potempkin*, *Berlin*, *Frankenstein,* and *Grand Hotel*.

Technical improvements continued to be made and a number of efforts were made to produce systems for projecting 3D films. In 1935 Dundonians had the chance to use red and green spectacles to see films in 3D when the **Kinnaird** screened a film in the 'Audioscopiks' system. It was said that they would "startle audiences when hands and feet came out of the screen, and a soda siphon threatened to soak the balcony." However most cinema goers did not like the spectacles and 3D pictures did not catch on.

Colour films had been around from very early on in the development of movies and were quite common in the days of silent films. However problems were encountered when combining existing techniques for producing coloured pictures with the inclusion of a sound track on the film. This led to the abandoning of colour films for the first years of talkies. It was not until the mid 30s that the first practical colour film system became widely available. This was the three colour Technicolor system and was the principal system used in the film industry until its monopoly was broken in the 1940s. The first film in three-colour Technicolor was an animated Walt Disney cartoon, *Flowers and Trees*, made in 1932, and the first feature film *Becky Sharp*, was released in 1935. More feature films began to be made in colour but it remained expensive, and it was only when the threat posed by television became plain in the 1950s that colour became the norm.

One cloud on the horizon was the decision in 1931 by the Government to impose an Entertainment Tax on cinema seats. On 17 March 1932 Harry Dickson, the manager of the **Forest Park Cinema** said at a meeting of the Scottish Cinematograph Exhibitors Association "the adverse effects in Dundee of the re-imposition of Entertainment Tax on cheaper seats has been on average a drop in attendances of 55%".

A mark of the growing scale of the cinema industry in Dundee was the holding, on 5th March 1935, of the first Annual Luncheon of the Dundee section of the Scottish branch of the Cinematograph Exhibitors Association. The event, as held in the **Royal British Hotel**, was addressed by Lord Provost Buist. The Lord Provost remarked on "the great assistance the cinema trade had given to the city, especially during the last few years, in the way of cheering up the unemployed".

The Second Annual Luncheon was addressed by Lord Provost Phin, who took a somewhat more positive view of the effects of film. He suggested that films had had a role in the raising of people's aspirations', "They brought home to the people the latest in clothes, the latest in hairdressing …. and the latest in housing. That, in turn, gave the populace the desire to improve their conditions".

He could have added that the cinemas also brought them the latest in crime, as during the 1930s gangster films like *Little Caesar* became very popular. Special effects films like *King Kong* and horror films like *Frankenstein* were also very successful. But in Dundee the picture that eclipsed all others for attendances was the Walt Disney full length animated *Snow White and the Seven Dwarfs* which led to enormous queues at the Odeon in 1938. It was subsequently shown at virtually every cinema in Dundee and even played for two weeks in the **Victoria** in 1970.

A further sign of the grip of films on the city was Arthur Henderson's attempt to turn back the clock in 1937 by the reintroduction of theatrical performances in the **Alhambra**. This failed and he was compelled to revert to showing films in 1939.

In the 1930s, films were advertised in the Courier, the Evening Telegraph and the Sporting Post, but there was still a kind of hierarchy at that time as only the major cinemas such as **The Playhouse**, **The Palace**, **The Kings**, **The Kinnnaird**, **La Scala**, **The Majestic** and **The Victoria** advertised in the Courier although all the cinemas advertised in the Evening Telegraph and the Sporting Post. But films had become central to a Dundonian's entertainment.

In July 1939, one could see a large article entitled 'Our Talkie Guide' in the Evening Telegraph while the Courier contained a four column wide spread entitled 'Cinema News and Reviews'. This was not all surprising as this year, saw the largest number of cinemas ever to operate simultaneously in Dundee. Those advertising in the Courier and the Evening Telegraph of 7th July were as follows: **The Kinnaird**, **The Majestic**, **Green's Playhouse**, **La Scala**, **The Plaza**, **The Kings**, **The Regent**, **The Royal**, **The Broadway**, **The Vic**, **The Palladium**, **The Forest Park**, **Grays**, **The Rialto**, **The Astoria**, **The Odeon**, **The Empire**, **The New Cinema**, **The Tivoli**, **The Royalty**, **The Cinerama**, **The Alhambra**, **The Princess**, **T**h**e Broughty Ferry Picture House** and **The Regal**, Broughty Ferry. In addition **The Britannia** was advertised as "closed for reconstuction". But alongside were advertisements for the distribution of gas masks and articles about air raid shelters.

As the number of cinemas increased, competition became fierce and some cinema owners came to the conclusion that advertising in the local press was not sufficient. Dundonians became used to publicity stunts as men dressed in gorilla costumes paraded through the city centre to advertise the screening of *King Kong* while others dressed in togas were on the march when yet another Roman epic was screened. On another occasion the police were less than happy when they responded to a report that a woman was drowning in the harbour only to find that the 'woman' was a cardboard cut out of Kay Kendall advertising a current film.

Laurel and Hardy

Mr Charles G. Caine remembers a particular stunt to publicise the screening of a film called *Covered Wagons*. A laundalette was obtained, steel hoops attached to the top and covered in canvas to form a covered wagon. He was then dressed as a cowboy, along with the rest of the staff, and given the task of driving the covered wagon through the City centre. Unfortunately the horse bolted, leaving the driver on his back in the body of the 'wagon', with the horse totally out of control. The escapade only ended when the horse got tired and came to a stop.

The Studio Star system

With the advent of talking pictures many of the favourite silent stars vanished, not only because of their voices, but also because the film studios were always looking for somebody new, somebody different.

The new stars were well publicised by the studios who attempted to create and package their stars according to the studio's particular ideas or fashions of the time. This created a situation where many moviegoers would go to see any film that featured their favourite stars, irrespective of the quality of the film. As the 30s progressed no advert for a film was complete without the names of leading stars.

As a result, a minor industry developed producing magazines, books, annuals and photos, all giving information on films and especially film stars. Staff were employed by all the major studios to deal with the vast amount of fan mail addressed to the stars. Autographed pictures were supplied to fans and some cinema chains, such as Associated British Cinema (ABC), published what they called film reviews but which were essentially film magazines. There was even a weekly comic, aimed at children, which was called 'Film Fun'.

With stars being so heavily promoted it was not surprising that virtually every filmgoer had their favourite stars. Norman Robertson recalled "My first love at the cinema was Dorothy Lamour, followed by Alice Fay and Patricia Roc." Alec McLeish remembers that Joan Crawford was his favourite and that my wife made sure we saw every film that starred Errol Flynn."

Playhouse staff

Staff

As cinema attendances and the cinemas themselves grew in size, cinemas employed doormen in uniform who controlled the queues and admittances and dealt with any disruptions or emergencies. **The King's**, **The Majestic**, **The Kinnaird**, **La Scala**, **The Playhouse**, **Forest Park**, the earlier **Electric Theatre**, Nethergate and the **New Grand**, King St, Broughty Ferry all employed doormen in their time. An earlier name was 'checker' either because the doormen checked the entrance tickets or checking the behaviour of patrons, especially the young at matinees. Sometimes the Manager, always in evening dress, appeared at the door to control the queues.

Green's Playhouse had large numbers of staff required to run it – almost 50 in all including managers, door men, cashiers, projectionists, usherettes, waitresses for the Tea-room and Sunshine Café, and staff for the Chocolate Box and Milk Bar.

The Second World War

After the declaration of war by the Britain on 3rd September 1939, the Government ordered all cinemas and theatres to close at once as they were afraid of the mass casualties that might be caused by bombs falling on crowded buildings. The ban did not last long and was rescinded with effect from 16th September 1939. Minnie Macintosh, the Chairwoman of the local association of cinema owners, expressed the relief not only of the owners, but the employees as well when she said "If this had gone on, over 400 jobs would have been lost". The Government had reassessed both the level of danger and the all too apparent effects on civilian morale and had had a change of heart. So deep did this go that, on Boxing Day 1939, the Government decided that cinemas would be allowed to open on Sundays. Naturally enough this did not apply to Scotland.

Queuing at
The Kinnaird.

Green's Playhouse
The Sunshine Café

THE SUNSHINE CAFE, (OPEN SUNDAYS 3 PM TILL 10 PM.)
GREENS PLAYHOUSE, NETHERGATE, DUNDEE.

During air raids, managers appeared on the stage to calm the audiences. No one was compelled to stay - the choice was theirs to go home or to air raid shelters- but the advice was 'Keep your heads - and your seats'. All cinemas had been made splinter proof and could be quickly emptied if necessary.

The Government was much quicker off the mark than in the First World War to realise the value of the cinema as a morale booster from the start. Although there were shortages of both materials and manpower, the government encouraged British studios to produce films which, although not propaganda, did support the war effort. Films such as *The Way Ahead* and *In Which We Serve* were good examples of this. Even Shakespeare was called into the breach with an intensely patriotic production of *Henry V* to which parties of school children were taken. Historical dramas were popular too and probably represented a way of getting away from the grimness of the present. Especially popular were the Gainsborough Studio melodramas such as *The Wicked Lady*. When the USA came into the war, the American studios also entered the field with popular films like *Mrs Miniver* and *Casablanca*.

Newsreels also focused on the war. Alex McLeish recalls seeing a Pathé newsreel showing the capture of German soldiers on the Lofoten Islands shortly before he went off the join the war himself.

On 4th March 1940, the **Regal** in Broughty Ferry did its bit for the war effort by opening a canteen for services personnel, whilst the Dundee Film Society played their role in entertaining the troops by putting on Sunday shows at **La Scala**. George Kinnear, Chairman of the Society interviewed in October 1948, recalled that sub titles were provided in five languages - French, Dutch, Norwegian, Polish, and, because some of the films were from abroad, English as well.

Dundonians' spirits were raised in 1940, when it was announced by the Green Brothers that they had negotiated a special deal to show *Gone with the Wind* at the **Playhouse**. The downside was that prices were raised to see the film. This, they alleged, was because of conditions imposed by the distributors. The minimum

prices were to be 3/6d for the matinees and 4/6d for the evening performances. It was a mark of the power of the distributors that the deal struck meant that they got £70 for each £100 taken at the box office.

During the war, cinema vans were deployed all over the United Kingdom both to encourage the war effort and to sell Savings Bonds. In Dundee, this occurred on a number of occasions, an example being the stationing for three days, of a cinema van in City Square on 19th August 1943. This made an impression on Jimmy Smith who recalls "As a young boy I was very impressed with the matt black interior. With no projection ray it was like magic".

Newsreels did their bit for the war effort by frequently giving advice on how to make do on the limited food that was available and how to recycle clothes – even how to make dresses from curtains! At another level, audiences sang along to a cartoon entitled *Run Rabbit Run* in which the rabbit had Hitler's head and the farmer with a gun was Winston Churchill. Truly propaganda had no bounds.

But not all Government efforts were focussed on the war. Social issues also raised their head and in 1944 a film entitled *Children of the City* was made in Dundee and subsequently screened throughout the UK. Its theme was juvenile delinquency and focussed on three boys convicted of robbery. The image was of an oppressive environment and substandard living conditions. The film was commissioned by the Government to publicise the work of Children's Panels which had recently been introduced. Its vision of Dundee was not exactly flattering, to say the least but it had a point to make and was well made by its directorial team of Paul Rotha and photographer Wolfgang Suschitzky.

The Post War Period

The immediate post war world was a cold and grey one in almost all respects. Britain was virtually bankrupt. Food and clothes rationing remained in force until the 1950s and there was an acute housing shortage.

Films were a refuge from those problems. Audiences, not surprisingly, queued to see Ealing Comedies such as *Whisky Galore, Kind Hearts and Coronets* from Britain, and films from America such as *It's a Wonderful Life* and *The Best Years of their Lives, Brief Encounter* and *The Third Man,* all of which were later regarded as classics, are still popular today.

There were at this time a significant number of employees in the cinema business in Dundee and the demand for projectionists in the 1950s resulted in the Dundee Trades College in Victoria Road running courses for apprentice projectionists.

Annual UK attendances averaged around one and a half billion over the period from 1945 to 1950. However by the end of this period, attendances had passed their peak dropping from 1.6 billion in 1945 to 1.4 billion in 1950. Although this was still well above the 900 million or so average attendances in the pre-war period, concerns were still being raised about the effects of Entertainment Tax on the viability of cinemas.

The studio owners had some cause to complain for the tax taken was £41 million out of a gross take of £115 million. In 1949, Arthur Rank, the most powerful person in the UK film industry was quite blunt. Unless the duty was reduced he would cease production in Britain. The tax was abolished the following year, but the cloud on the horizon that was the development of television would prove to be much more of a problem than that posed by the Entertainment Tax.

Queuing to get into
the Green's Playhouse

Going to the movies

Going to the movies was always an exciting experience and never more so than in the 1930s and 1940s. Deciding when and where to go could take some time, and usually depended upon your circumstances at work. Shift workers would often be found in afternoon performances. Those waiting to see the second evening performances referred to the movie-goers coming out of the cinema as they went in as "early bedders". Going outwith Friday and Saturday nights would greatly improve your chances of getting in to see more popular films. Films showing at the larger city centre cinemas were advertised in the Courier but the films available at all the cinemas were set out in the Evening Telegraph which also ran regular columns of reviews of the latest films.

But newspapers were not the only method of advertising. The out-of-centre-cinemas were very much tied into their neighbourhood, with readily recognised patrons visiting more than once a week. Posters for the coming films were distributed to local shops who were given tickets for the cinema, but these were not to be used on Friday or Saturday nights.

Mrs Hannah Farrell recalled, "we went to the **Forest Park Picture House** regularly on Mondays and Thursdays with my cousins and my aunt Maryanne. The admission price was 4d (2p). On Tuesday I might go with my mum to the **Astoria** or the **Alhambra**, but with my uncle on Fridays or Saturdays to **The Scala** or **The Kings**".

Anticipation was heightened before the visit by passing posters in local shop windows or on hoardings with coloured images depicting perhaps a murder, a Broadway show or maybe an attack by pirates. Almost always there was a well developed girl in a revealing dress.

Practically all movie-goers at this time arrived by bus or on foot. Queuing was the norm for popular films. This was not just the case in Dundee. In America the word 'blockbuster' was coined to indicate that a film was so popular that queues stretched right around a city block.

Green's Playhouse
programme from 1937

42

Eventually one arrived at a cashier's desk that could vary from the miniscule in the smaller cinemas, to something much grander in the larger movie houses. Sometimes, as in the **Cinerama**, there were separate cash desks for the cheaper and the more expensive seats.

When you entered the auditorium there was nearly always a haze of cigarette smoke. If the film was well attended, this would be sufficiently thick to render visible a cone of light between the projector and the screen. Usherettes with a torch would conduct you to a vacant seat. The rear rows were invariably full of courting couples although these could be found anywhere in the darkened space. To facilitate their togetherness, a number of cinemas installed chummy seats which would take two people. The best example in Dundee was **Green's Playhouse** with its golden divans, known in some quarters as 'the golden dive-ons'. Ashtrays were provided on the backs of seats in front of you.

Programmes

In the early days films ran for only two or three days but popular films then began to be screened for a whole week. Initially the town centre cinemas showed four screenings a day at 2.30, 4.30, 6.30 and 8.30pm. Later, they showed continuously. The out-of-centre-cinemas usually showed at fixed times.

Continuous showing led to one of the more curious experiences associated with movie-going. One could, and many did, go into the cinema at any time and thus often arrive in the middle of a film. One then had to pick up the plot while seeing the rest of the film, watch the second feature, and a newsreel and trailers, and then finally see the first part of the film that had been showing when one entered. It seems strange now but was commonplace then.

The programme would normally start with the B movie and be followed by a newsreel and a cartoon. The cartoons were virtually all from America and, initially at least, nearly all made by Walt Disney. However it is unlikely that many Dundee moviegoers realised that the voice of Disney's Mickey Mouse was being provided by Dundonian James (Jimmy) McDonald.

There would be a short interval in which usherettes would appear and sell cigarettes and ice cream. (In passing it is interesting to note that when the **Cinerama** was sold by the Pennycooks to J. B. Milne the profits from the ice cream were almost as much as the profits from ticket sales.) Then the main feature would follow.

The end of the main feature was marked by a somewhat unseemly rush to get to the exits, rather than to stay and stand while the National Anthem was played to end the night's proceedings.

Saturday Cinema

If, on the other hand, you were a youngster, you might well have gone to special performances that were laid on for children on Saturday mornings or afternoons. These could be a somewhat noisy experience as cheering of heroes and hissing of villains was the norm rather than the exception. Minor scuffles often occurred, only to be quelled by usherettes using their torches to identify the guilty.

Bert Carr later recalled "One of my fond memories of movies was that I belonged to the **Odeon** and the **Empire** Cinema Clubs, and on my birthday each year I got the birthday card which allowed me into the movies FREE. It was a good job the **Odeon** showed its pictures on Saturday morning and the Empire on Saturday afternoon. Except for rushing home for 'denner' between the shows I could spend almost the whole day at the pictures FREE".

James (Jimmy) McDonald

The ABC Saturday
morning song

Some of the cinema chains made special efforts in this regard. **The Gaumont** was one of these and established a children's club. Proceedings opened with a song which many Dundonians will recall:

> *"We come along on Saturday Morning Greeting everybody with a smile*
> *We come along on Saturday morning Knowing its all worth while*
> *As members of the G B Club We all intend to be*
> *Good citizens when we grow up and champion of the free".*

If you had gone to the **ABC** then it would have been the Children's Matinee where you would have sung:

> *"We are the boys and girls well known as Minors of the ABC,*
> *And every Saturday we all line up to see the films we like and shout aloud with glee,*
> *We laugh and have our sing song, such a happy crowd are we*
> *We're all pals together, we are the Minors of the ABC".*

The City Council became worried about the tone of some of the pictures shown and took action in November 1934, when the Dundee Juvenile Organisations Committee established an experimental children's cinema. This was the first in Scotland and the screenings took place at the **Cinerama** in Tay Street. The first showing consisted of a comedy film, a newsreel, and three or four short films endorsed by the Committee. The ultimate fate of this initiative is unknown but there is no trace of it after the Second World War.

Children's pictures
at the Princess

6

The Movie Moguls of Dundee

Given the great popularity of the movies, and the consequent large numbers of cinemas in Dundee, it is not altogether surprising that individuals emerged who owned significant numbers of movie houses. In Dundee the two most important of these were the Pennycook family and J. B. Milne.

The Pennycooks - a family affair

The 'Pennycook' family was involved with the development of the cinema in Dundee from the earliest years. John Pennycook was born in 1860 and had five sons and three daughters. He was described by family members as a quiet and couthie man. His sons, Robert, William, Thomson, Roger and Matthew, and his daughters, Euphemia, Jane and Isobel, all at some time worked in the cinema business in Dundee and elsewhere in Scotland.

The Pennycook family Back: William, Roger Robert Matthew Front: John, Thomson, Euphemia, Jane, Isobel, Mary

John Pennycook had a Hansom Cab, which operated from a stance between the Western and Taybridge stations. His eldest son, Robert (1882-1975), bought Peter Feathers' collapsible film booth in William Street in 1908. He took on his father as cashier in this family venture, which at various times employed all the brothers. Bought for £60, it had at one time housed a carnival Hall of Mirrors. Robert later described it, not surprisingly, as 'a ramshackle affair' as it consisted of four collapsible wooden walls and a canvas roof. The seats were just wooden planks balanced on metal drums with performances lasting about an hour. Whilst it was supposed to be portable, it was only moved once when Robert took it to Perth, but he soon took it back to Dundee where the audiences were bigger.

Thomson was from the start the most technically minded of the family and was very proficient at handling and repairing all kinds of cinematic equipment. The youngest son, Matthew, when still a schoolboy, was employed as the 'chocolate boy' in charge of sweet sales. Thus began an entertainment dynasty in the city that was to last for almost sixty years.

The second Electric Theatre with Matthew and Jane Pennycook

In 1912, the family moved forward on two fronts. First they converted an old church hall and opened it as **The Magnet Picture** and **Variety Palace** at 8 Well Road, off Hawkhill. In the same year John Pennycook bought the **Electric Theatre** in the Nethergate from Peter Feathers and used the premises to run one reel films. William and Roger worked there.

At the same time they operated from premises in Perth and soon they accumulated sufficient capital to contemplate building a cinema of their own. So in 1913, after selling the first **Electric Theatre** in William Street, the Pennycooks opened the **Pavilion Picture Theatre** at 67 Alexander Street. This they had had literally built themselves with aid of subcontractors.

The **Pavilion** was a substantial building, having some 950 seats and was run by Roger and his father John Pennycook. In 1920 they refurbished and renamed it as **The Palladium Picture House**. To many of its local patrons it was familiarly known as 'The Plad' or 'The Peek'.

The advent of the First World War put a halt to their plans as Robert was sent to France. There he worked as a projectionist in a government tent theatre, provided as entertainment for the troops. Thomson joined the Royal Engineers but, found to have TB, was discharged in 1915 and returned to Dundee to help in the **Electric Theatre** in the Nethergate. William played his part in the war and he served as a despatch rider with the Royal Engineers. During this time, he was shot in the foot which left him with a permanent limp.

In 1918 Robert, who was described by family members as "always the more adventurous of the brothers" and "very active", moved to Glasgow as the manager of the Wellington Palace in Commercial Road. This he bought in 1928 from J. J. Bennell and remodelled it as a 1900 seat cinema, the architect being A. V. Gardner. He also acquired other cinemas, notably the Tonic in Rutherglen, The Cinema in Balfron, and the Magnet and the Ritz in Gourock.

The Pennycooks seem to have been quite outward looking as Thomson and Robert decided to put on film shows in a hall in Falkirk, perhaps just to see whether there was an opportunity to set up a business there. This started disastrously as, on the very first night the film caught fire and they had to reimburse all the customers. After this it was very late and without the generosity of one of the ushers they

Robert Pennycook

In front of the Cinerama - from the Horse's mouth

would have been out on the street. Fortunately he gave them a bed for the night and the usher's family and the Pennycooks became very close friends.

Their next project was very different. In 1918, the Pennycooks rented what had been a Gaelic Chapel in South Tay Street and as the **Tay Street Cinema,** used it to show films. In 1922, they bought the premises, then in 1923 converted the former church into a cinema and opened it as the **Cinerama**. In the course of this they added a balcony and, when very young, Robert Pennycook Jnr remembered seeing an iron girder being swung into the building to form part of the reconstruction. He recalled how the Blackness trams were halted to allow this manoeuvre to take place.

Members of the Pennycook family recalled that the **Cinerama** was plagued with mice and that a cat and a terrier were used to keep them down. In 1925 the **Royalty Kinema**, located on the site of the former **Edenbank Picture House** in Watson Street, became the next cinema purchased by the firm. It was in this picture house in 1926 (along with the **Cinerama** and the **Rialto Kinema**) that the first short 'talkies' were heard and seen in Dundee. In 1928, the first full length feature film with passages of dialogue and singing - *The Jazz Singer* was shown at the **Royalty Kinema**, the premiere being attended by the then Lord and Lady Airlie.

By the late I920s, father John and all five Pennycook sons were active in the cinema business but John died in February 1936 aged 76 years leaving his sons Matthew and Roger jointly in charge of the **Cinerama**.

In 1939, William had acquired premises in Albert Street (sited where the Co-op store now stands) intending to build a modern cinema, but this project did not go ahead because of building restrictions imposed during and after the war. After the end of the restrictions in the 1950s the advent of television meant that the project was abandoned.

Just before World War Two, the Pennycooks acquired the **New Cinema** in Morgan Street and, in 1940, the **Alhambra** in Bellfield Street, which they renamed **The State**. Thomson and his son Robert ran the **New Cinema** but Robert joined the Royal Air Force.

The Royalty Kinema
Watson Street

The cinema business boomed in the war years and William, with the assistance principally of the wives of the family, ran successful Saturday afternoon and evening shows in the **Caird Hall**, such was the demand for picture-going. In 1945, when fire severely damaged their Morgan Street cinema, Thomson suffered burns on his hands and face in an attempt to put the fire out. After reconstruction it reopened in 1948 but when in 1959 the **Royalty Kinema** and the **State** were sold to the J. B. Milne chain, brothers Thomson and William decided to retire.

William Pennycook died in May 1960. However, Thomson returned to join his brothers Matthew and Roger at the **Cinerama** until it was demolished in 1964.

The Royalty Kinema
Orchestra and staff

The Palladium as The Rex

After the family business was sold to J. B. Milne, Matthew became the manager of the **Ritz** cinema in Morgan Street. He was working there when he died in July 1965.

Robert was always interested in technology and in his retirement he experimented with projection lenses. In 1969, he patented a lens which produced a three dimensional effect. Robert Pennycook died in March 1975 at the age of 92.

Thomson Pennycook died in September 1979 and the last of the brothers, Roger, died in March 1996 at the age of 97.

The Pennycooks were a remarkable family whose story is an integral part of the history of cinema in Dundee.

J. B. Milne - a self made man

J. B. Milne was born John Bannerman McLeod Milne in September 1902. He was born in Ellen Street, his father being Charles Milne a coal merchant in the city. J. B. had an elder sister, Elizabeth, and a younger brother Charles. Before he was ten he had taken up the violin.

His first ambition was earn his fortune by going to India, but his mother told him that he was far too young and that for the time being he should get on with his violin lessons. He started work as a mill mechanic and soon exhibited the energy that would characterise his whole life.

By the time he was 16 he was working for twelve hours during the day at the Dura Works, then teaching violin for two hours in the evening, after which he went on to work until midnight as a violinist in a dance hall. Music and the theatre clearly interested J. B. more than his work in the textile mill and he eventually became what he wryly referred to as "the musical director and cleaner" at the **Royalty Kinema** for the princely sum of nineteen shillings a week.

Ever hard working and ambitious, he lived off the £3 per week that he earned at the mill and saved everything else. He invested his savings in a car rental firm, which

The County, Kinross

Opening programme for the Brit

he sold in 1928. With the capital he was able to buy his first cinema, the **Palladium**, from Heyman Cohen.

At that time the **Palladium** did not have individual seats, just long benches. It was not unusual for people to be pushed onto one end of the bench by the usher, causing unsuspecting patrons to be pushed off the far end. Later the **Palladium** was renamed as the **Rex** - the name of J. B.'s Labrador dog.

In some ways it was fortunate for him that he bought his first cinema in 1928 at a particularly crucial point in the history of moving pictures. The very next year 'Talkies' came to Dundee. He was quick to realise the potential of sound movies when many other cinema owners regarded them as a fad and thought that they would never really catch on. J. B. was certain that they would and installed the necessary equipment in the **Palladium**. This gave him a good start in the cinema business and, as soon as possible, he proceeded to acquire more cinemas.

J. B. Milne's next acquisition was the **Picture House**, Tayport, which he acquired in 1931. The **Picture House** had 453 seats and was equipped with a splendid vertical neon sign.

For his next cinema J. B. looked for a site closer to the city centre and found it in Victoria Road where in 1933 he acquired the **Victoria Cinema**. He carried out extensive improvements before the official opening by Lord Provost Buist took place in 1935.

After 1934, he built the Regal Cinema in Blairgowrie and sold it to a company of which he was the chairman.

In 1936, he took over the **Britannia Cinema** in Smalls Wynd in Dundee. Briefly renamed by Milne as the '**Brit**', it was upgraded three years later in 1939 and renamed the **Regal**.

J. B. was always ambitious and his ambitions were never going to be confined locally. It was therefore not surprising that he soon began to venture much further afield. In March 1938, he formed a company to acquire land in Kinross for a new cinema. The **County**, as it was named, was built on Station Road and opened on 12th September 1938. Originally, the cinema had a capacity of 600 but later this was reduced to about 400 to avoid Entertainment Tax.

Jimmy Brown and Alec Wright with usherettes at The Kinnaird promoting 'Gigi'

J. B. Milne with his Rolls Royce at Ruthven House

Typical of cinema programming of its day, the opening bill had three elements. These consisted of a British Movietone newsreel, Shirley Temple in *Heidi*, and *The Jones Family in Hot Water*. Adult ticket prices ranged from 6d in the stalls to 1/3d for the balcony. Children's prices were 4d to 9d.

J. B. was determined that his new cinema would be as up to date as he could make it. At its opening the County was described as "both dignified and modern in design. Internally it is constructed according to the latest scientific principles to ensure than every patron, no matter where seated, will have perfect and strainless vision of the screen and hear every word of dialogue and note of music without distortion."

Milne was very active in 1938 and the Courier reported on July 20 that not only had his new cinema in Blairgowrie just opened that week, but work was about to start on his eighth cinema. This was the Regal in Peterhead which subsequently opened in January 1939. It was a 1,500 seat cinema that incorporated a café, a dance hall and four shops, and was built for a cost of some £25,000.

In December 1938, together with Minnie MacIntosh, he submitted a proposal for a cinema on the north side of Arbroath Road. However this was rejected by the City Council. Thwarted in this aim, in 1939 he acquired the **Broadway** in Arthurstone Terrace. This was a bold step, given that by this time another major war was generally seen as inevitable.

However the period of the Second World War saw J. B. Milne energetically expanding his cinema chain. In 1941, he acquired the Cinema in McDuff, which he refurbished and opened as the Regal; the Picture House in Banff, which he also renamed as the Regal, the Scala in Cupar and the Regal in Auchterarder.

In 1944, he acquired the **Kinnaird** in Bank Street from the Hamilton brothers.

By the end of World War Two, J. B. had become a man of some substance owning over a dozen cinemas. This was reflected in his purchase in 1946 of the 32 roomed

51

mansion and the associated 1,000 acre estate of Ruthven near Meigle, in Perthshire. And for a man in his position a Rolls Royce seemed to be the car to drive.

The post war period

The Playhouse/Capitol/
Kingsway/Pavilion,
Galashiels

It was in the period after the end of the war and particularly the 1950s that JB Milne really spread his wings. During this decade he acquired or built some 12 cinemas in Dundee, Dunfermline, Methil, East Wemyss, Montrose, Peterhead, Arbroath, and Galashiels.

The North Star in Lerwick on Shetland was the most northerly of J. B.'s cinemas and was acquired by him just after the end of World War 2. The cinema had a nominal capacity of 600 but Charlie Milne recalls that 'when really popular films were being shown the stairways were, quite illegally, covered with seated patrons.'

Milne decided in the mid 1950s to build a major new cinema on a site in the Seagate. This site had been formerly occupied by the **Majestic Cinema** which had been burnt down during the war. The new cinema was to be the **Capitol**, which opened in 1956. The **Capitol** was the first cinema in Dundee that was constructed specifically to accommodate CinemaScope films with their wide picture ratio

The Capitol

However within 3 years J. B. had sold it to the Associated British Cinemas chain. Odd though this must have seemed to some, the sale was part of a much bigger deal as J. B. M. gained ownership of four cinemas from the ABC chain. J. B. bullishly stated in 1959, "We have sold 1,300 seats and acquired 3,000". But there may have been other reasons for the disposal of this new cinema. Alex Reid, who worked for J. B. Milne recalls "I have heard that J. B. M. was never happy with the **Capitol**, either as a building or as a business. Apparently there were difficulties booking attractive new films. He was, seemingly, not altogether unhappy to dispose of the building to ABC."

Milne's acquisitions as his part of the deal included the Plaza and Kings in Montrose, formerly leased by J. B. M. from ABC and the Playhouse in Galashiels. Not a man

J. B. MILNE Joins with

THE MANAGEMENT & STAFFS OF

J. B. MILNE THEATRES LTD.

and

THE ALL SQUARE BINGO CLUB

In Wishing All Patrons and Members

A Merry Christmas and A Happy and Prosperous New Year

ALL SQUARE BINGO CLUBS

PLAZA	Dundee	OPERA HOUSE	Lochgelly	PICTURE HOUSE	Banff
STATE	Dundee	PALACE	Methil	REGAL	Macduff
BROADWAY	Dundee	CAPITOL	Galashiels	REGAL	Blairgowrie
PALACE	Arbroath	TUDOR	Edinburgh	SCALA	Cupar
KING'S	Montrose	REGENT	Leven	NORTH STAR	Lerwick
PICTURE HOUSE	Cowdenbeath	REGAL	Peterhead	PLAYHOUSE	Stornoway

CINEMAS

PLAZA	Dundee	PICTURE HOUSE	Cowdenbeath	PICTURE HOUSE	Banff
ROYALTY	Dundee	OPERA HOUSE	Lochgelly	REGAL	Blairgowrie
RITZ	Dundee	IMPERIAL	Methil	SCALA	Cupar
STATE	Dundee	CAPITOL	Galashiels	PICTURE HOUSE	Tayport
VICTORIA	Dundee	ASTORIA	Edinburgh	NORTH STAR	Lerwick
PALACE	Arbroath	TIVOLI	Edinburgh	PLAYHOUSE	Stornoway
PLAYHOUSE	Montrose	TROXY	Leven	COUNTY	Kinross
		PLAYHOUSE	Peterhead		

to waste anything J. B. M. removed the **CAPITOL** sign from the Seagate cinema, transported it to Galashiels and the Playhouse became the Capitol. The Playhouse/Capitol was a substantial building, it was first built as a theatre and opened in 1920. The property contained 5 shops, a restaurant and a dance hall.

By 1957, J. B. Milne, who owned over 20 cinemas, was a person to be reckoned with in the Scottish cinema scene. As a sign of this his company was involved with the Summer Conference of the Cinema Exhibitors Association at Gleneagles. He refurbished his Auchterarder cinema especially for a visit by the conference delegates.

In 1958 he acquired the **Plaza**, Hilltown, from ABC for £30,500. At the time this 1,500 seat cinema was the largest cinema in his empire, which was still a privately owned company.

He followed this in 1959 by buying the **Stobswell Cinema** Theatre (which he renamed the **Ritz**), the **Royalty** and the **State** from the Pennycook family. His nephew Charles, who followed J. B. M. into the cinema business, recalls that when his uncle purchased the **Royalty** from the Pennycook chain, he took him to the theatre, walked down to where the orchestra pit had been, banged the floor with his stick, and proclaimed - "This is where I used to play". Nostalgic he may have been, but his first action was to renovate the cinema, including the replacement of its seating.

In the same year J. B. M. did a deal with Caledonian Associated Cinemas. He acquired the Angus Playhouse, Montrose, and the Playhouse, Peterhead from CAC who took the Ritz, Crieff and the Alhambra, Dunfermline in exchange, thus ensuring neither exhibitor was in direct competition in any town.

Curtains from Montrose were taken to equip Blairgowrie, which Alex Braid recalls, had as its first Manager Davie Stewart. The cinema had a riverside location and all the balcony was furnished with chummy seats.

During the late 1950s, he took over the Empire in East Wemys and renamed it, as usual, the Regal. At this time there was a significant and continuing decline in British cinema-going. Hardest hit were cinemas in smaller communities where many of J. B.'s movie houses were located. Always alert to change, with the onset of the 1960s, Milne saw that cinema attendances were beginning to decline. Recognising the potential of bingo he introduced it into his cinemas. Some of his cinemas continued to show films, some became bingo halls and some combined the two functions. In 1966, 9 of his 31 properties had both bingo and cinema whilst the rest were fairly evenly split between movie houses and bingo halls.

The 1960s
His energy showed no signs of abating. In October 1961 he acquired the 1,000 seat Troxy in Leven and the 800 seat Imperial in Methil where he already owned the Palace. Then he turned his attention to the capital, buying three substantial cinemas in Edinburgh - the Tudor, the Astoria and the Tivoli. Alex Braid recalls, "the Tudor, which had been a former drill hall, was a ghastly cinema. A particular problem was the placing of the projector room on the balcony which lead to passing patrons' shadows appearing on the screen".

His last acquisitions were the **Regal**, Broughty Ferry, which he bought from the Arbroath Cinema Company in 1968 along with the Picture House, Arbroath.

J. B. M. the business man
James B. Milne had started his working life being employed by others; now, as his empire grew, the boot was on the other foot, as he was responsible for an ever increasing number of workers. His approach to his business was to involve his family and both his brother and sister were employed by the firm. He insisted that everyone had to work their way up through the business and so it was with his nephew, Charlie Milne. When he joined the firm, it was firstly as an electrician's labourer and then as a projectionist. However he soon became a problem solver sent to cinemas where things had gone wrong. He then became a manager before being promoted to a circuit supervisor.

Charlie's memories of his uncle give a good idea of his boss's management style. J. B. had an obsession with detail and was totally dedicated to succeeding in the business. He always insisted that he was right no matter what the circumstances, but he was very quiet and did not lose his temper. His oft stated axiom was "Not money – profitability". For example he would analyse the day's takings from all the cinemas every night looking for anomalies or signs of problems. It has to be said that on this front J. B. M. was very secretive. So much so that managers had to use what he called the Davenport's code when reporting their takings over the phone. In this code each letter of Davenports stood for a figure – D equalled 1, A equalled 2, and so on. However the telephonists (who were not supposed to be in the know) soon worked things out and knew exactly what had been taken in any particular cinema.

But for J .B. security was not the only matter that had to be dealt with. Staff management was a case in point. At that time, cinemas were licensed by the local authority. As the manager needed to be named as the licensee, the choice of manager was important to J. B. At another level, the company policy covered matters of conduct. If any of the male staff got any of the usherettes pregnant their

The Tudor
Edinburgh

fate depended on their marital status. If the man was single, he was shifted to another cinema, if the offender was married he was sacked.

But the world of cinema at that time was far different to the world of multi screen complexes and art house cinemas we have today. Many of the cinemas were converted from variety or dance halls and at that time it was quite common for cinemas to put on variety acts. Charlie Milne remembers a singing and dancing troupe called the Moxon Girls. The leader, May Moxon, was a solo star and often appeared in a dinner jacket a la Marlene Deitrich.

The staff all wore uniforms, and the usherettes were detailed to waft perfume from pressurised containers to improve the ambience in J. B.'s cinemas.

It was the 1950s before J. B. made Charlie Milne the temporary manager at the Ritz. The first film to be shown at the Ritz when he was manager was *Burke and Hare*. Charlie decided to do something special and sent out invitations to the first night to all the Burkes and Hares he could find in the local telephone directory. And to make it a special occasion he borrowed a skeleton from the University, got hold of a gravestone, and displayed them both in the cinema under a green floodlight. It really brought the people in, especially as the Sunday Post and the Dundee Courier did special articles on his efforts. However J. B. Milne's response was characteristic of his inimitable managerial style; he docked Charlie's wages for the amount spent sending the invitations to the Burkes and Hares as he had not authorised the expenditure.

Not altogether surprisingly, Charlie thought J. B. was a hard boss. On the other hand he was a thoroughly sociable man who loved visitors.

His desire for economy was always at the front of his mind. For example, he was never happy about the fact that he had to pay for trailers for coming films. Not unreasonably, he felt that they should be supplied free by the film distributors.

55

There were of course other kinds of problems to be faced. Charlie recalls that on one occasion at the **Ritz**, a 5 reel western was shown as reels 1, 2, 4, 3, 5 in that order, leaving the customers somewhat confused.

A more exotic example occurred at the **Victoria Cinema** that, from time to time, hosted theatrical events on its stage. When J. B. found himself with an unanticipated gap in his programme for the '**Vic**' due to a late cancellation by Harry Lauder he engaged a circus for a week. The stage had to be strengthened to take the weight of the elephants. That worked fine, but an unanticipated problem was that one of the elephants managed to redesign a blue and cream car, parked just outside the cinema, by the simple process of sitting on its bonnet. The car belonged to J. B. M.

The End of an Era

Mr J. B. Milne, originally a mill-boy with ambition, died at his home, Ruthven House, Meigle, on 24th September in 1968. Aged 66, he was the head of Scotland's largest privately owned cinema chain. When he died, he still controlled 34 cinemas and bingo halls from Bannerman House, his head office in South Tay Street. How did he do it? When interviewed by the Sunday Post in the 1950s he said "I was always ready to take a chance but I don't take risks".

He remained a real Dundonian all his days. Not only did he keep his head office in the city but in 1961 he initiated the 'Citizen of the Year' award which has been given by the City Council for annual presentation ever since. J. B. Milne even had a 32 bar reel written in his memory. The music was written by Angus Fitchet who dedicated it to 'J. B. Milne the man who gave me my start in my show business career'.

His work with cinemas spanned the era from the end of silent films, through the immense popularity of films in the 30s, 40s, and 50s, and ended at a time when the effects of television were causing cinema closures throughout the country. At its peak J. B. M.'s empire comprised cinemas in locations as far apart as Stornaway and Galashiels. However, despite building up a chain which had at its peak almost 40 cinemas, these were all in the east or the north of Scotland and never in the west of the country.

After his death, the business was taken over by Kingsway Entertainments Ltd. who were based in Kirkcaldy. For some time they continued to run the business under its name of J. B. Milne Theatres Ltd. But the chain so carefully built up was sold off piece by piece for other uses and today nothing but a memory remains of J. B. M.'s cinema empire.

JBM's Cinerama Star

From Boom to Bust and back again

7

As the 1950s progressed. Britain, and Dundee in particular, was changing fast. In the immediate post war period, the Government's first response to the housing crisis was to build prefabricated homes on small infill sites. But in the early 1950's this was followed right across Britain by enormous programmes of municipal housing. In Dundee these were located on the outskirts of the city. This led to a significant move of population away from the inner city where most cinemas were located.

If this was not bad enough for the cinema industry, social changes were taking place that changed matters significantly. Television, which had been growing very slowly, came into much more general use with the televising of the Coronation in 1953. In the UK, TV licences issued rose from 4.5 million in 1955 to 17.5 million in 1975. Over the same period, the number of cinemas in the UK dropped from 4,483 to 1,971. Cinemas reacted to falling profits by raising ticket prices above the rate of inflation. As a consequence, the increasing expense of a cinema visit became another factor in the decline of cinema going.

In the 1950's home entertainment became more available, with huge surges in the number of gramophone records being bought by young people. Personal portable radios tuned into current pop music programmes were increasingly found in teenage bedrooms. Quite simply there were more things to do than go to the cinema.

The result was that cinema attendances fell from 1.365 billion in 1950 to 500 million in 1960. The two major UK cinema chains, the Rank Organisation and the Associated British Picture Corporation started to close cinemas in large numbers. In 1956 Rank closed 79 of its cinemas and, in 1957, the ABC chain closed 65 of their movie houses. In a surprising irony the 1950s was the decade in which out of the top 12 box office films in the UK, 8 were British, something never experienced before and never to be repeated.

But Britain was not alone in experiencing a decline in cinema going. In the USA cinema attendances were also rapidly declining and dropped by over 50% between the end of the war and 1960. France saw a similar 50% drop in a ten year period.

The response of the film industry was to try anything that would differentiate cinema-going from watching television at home. One approach was to make films bigger and more colourful. The epic scale of films such as *Lawrence of Arabia*, *Dr Zhivago*, and *Ryan's Daughter* were good examples of this.

Different film formats were another response. *The Robe* which was screened in the **Regal** Broughty Ferry in 1954, was the first example to appear in Dundee of the Cinemascope wide screen system which proved popular. In 1952, **Green's Playhouse** featured *Metroscope*, an MGM 3D presentation, including *Third Dimensional Murder*. Later, in 1955, Hollywood produced *Bwana Devil*, the first US commercial 3D film. This was followed by a swathe of others but after the first flush of enthusiasm 3D films proved less popular. In 1958, 3D production stopped in Hollywood and 3D films dropped out of favour. Todd AO came to Dundee in 1959 when *South Pacific* was shown in the opening at the **ABC** in the Seagate.

Another approach was to present things that would not be allowed on television. Blood and gore were at the top of the list. When Hammer Films gained a world wide success with *The Curse of Frankenstein* in 1957, they set a pattern which would be

The giant Todd AO screen at the ABC

followed by others. Nevertheless films aimed at family audience continued to be popular and films like *Mary Poppins* and *The Sound of Music* were very successful.

In spite of all this and having erected new peripheral housing estates in the city, cinemas began to close. **The Queens** in Well Road closed in 1956. Following a fire in 1957, the **Empire** in Rosebank Street closed for good and in 1957 **Gray's Cinema** closed its doors for the last time.

Things were to get worse for the cinema industry. As the 1950s came to an end the municipal authorities across Britain turned their attention to the comprehensive redevelopment of the inner areas of their cities. This meant that, in the 1960s when substandard housing was cleared, the cinemas located in these areas were demolished at the same time.

This was very much the pattern in Dundee. In 1959, the **Princess Cinema** in the Hawkhill was closed and demolished to allow for the expansion of Dundee University. A similar fate overtook the **Regal** in Smalls Wynd. In 1963 **The Rex** was closed and demolished as part of the Alexander Street Comprehensive Development Area whilst the **Cinerama** in Tay Street was demolished in 1964 by the City Council to make way for a car park. The Watson Street CDA brought about the final closure saw the removal of the **Royalty Kinema**. **The Kinnaird** went in the mid 1960s when it was demolished to make way for the Overgate Shopping development. It was also a shopping development that saw the end of **La Scala**, which was bought and removed by F. W. Woolworths to allow for the expansion of their Murraygate premises.

In the late 1960s, faced with a stock of large cinemas that could no longer be filled, the reaction of the major chains was to consolidate. One way of doing this was to close the older and smaller cinemas and subdivide the larger, better placed ones. The principal example of this in Dundee was the conversion of the **ABC** in the Seagate to a two screen cinema. However, such efforts were not wholly successful due to another change taking place in the world outside the cinema industry. This was the rapid growth in car ownership, which meant that the lack of parking at the

inner city cinemas was another reason not to quit the television in the living room for a visit to the cinema.

Attendances continued to fall throughout the 1960s and, inevitably, the closures continued. In 1961, **The Royal** in Arthurstone Terrace went over to bingo. The **Regent Picture House** in Main Street ceased to show pictures in 1962 and went over to bingo, and in the same year the **Rialto** in Lochee was closed. In the following twelve months the **Broadway** went over to bingo, and the **Reres Cinema** in Broughty Ferry closed. The latter part of the decade saw two more closures - the **Forest Park Cinema** in 1967 and the surprising demise as a cinema of the once mighty **Green's Playhouse** in 1968.

During the 1970s, film makers began to concentrate their efforts on younger audiences, particularly the young male. Films were focused on the kind of thrills which could not be created on television. What also couldn't be done on television, was the special effects epic such as *Star Wars* and *Close Encounters of the Third Kind*.

In addition, a growingly permissive society also provided an area where TV could not compete with films. As Bill Murray, a retiring cinema manager, noted in 1976, "audiences are only interested in films with X certificates. It seems that Dundonians are only interested in sex and violence and it is our job to give it to them."

Nevertheless in the 1970s cinema attendances in the UK fell again, from 193 million in 1970 to 101 million in 1979. These resulted in more closures in Dundee. 1973 saw the closures of both the **Ritz** and the very much more upmarket **Odeon** in Strathmartine Road. Later, in 1977, the **Astoria** and the **Tivoli** also closed as cinemas.

The decline in the number of cinemas had implications for all of those providing services to them. At this time the distribution of films to cinemas in Dundee was carried out by The Film Transport Service (FTS) which provided film transport services to cinema operators and film distributors all over Britain. In Scotland, the company operated from depots in Aberdeen, Broxburn, Dundee, Dunfermline and Glasgow. In Dundee, FTS used four distinctive black and red coloured vans to transport films to the cinemas from their depot at Fairfield House in Liff Road, Lochee. With the decline in the number of cinemas the Dundee depot closed in the late 70s, and by the 1980s the company's sole distribution branch for the whole of Scotland was Broxburn. The final demise of the company in Scotland was not without its drama as Alex Braid recalls:

"Around 1983, I received a telephone call from the lady who managed the FTS operations in Scotland. She told me the company had gone bust and was ceasing operations! FTS had keys to every cinema in Scotland to allow their drivers to deliver and collect films during the night. She suggested I come immediately to Broxburn to collect these keys before she closed up.

I duly drove through to Broxburn where the said lady presented me with an enormous bunch of keys - hundreds - none of them labeled. I asked which keys were for which cinemas. She told me she had no idea - "the drivers know which is which and they've all been paid off!"

The next day I contacted all cinema owners in Scotland and we made alternative arrangements with a carrier called Courier Express. All cinemas were asked to provide new, labeled keys. I put the redundant keys in a large bag, took it down to the river Clyde where I chucked it in.

To this day, the keys to all cinemas operating in Scotland during the 1980s are at the bottom of the Clyde."

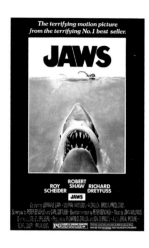

The 1970s were not all bad news. The blockbusters produced by the studios could still pull the Dundonians out on some occasions. In January 1977, *Jaws* was so popular in Dundee that it generated probably the only film - related riot to occur in the city. This occurred at the **Victoria** where the queue to see the film was so great that that the doors were closed leaving some hundreds outside. The irate crowd promptly rioted and the police had to be called in to sort things out.

There had also always been a demand for what could be loosely termed, art films. As cinema audiences grew smaller they became more discriminating. From the 1950s onwards, there had been a development of the market for art house films and for cinemas in which to show them. Given the tradition of cinema going in Dundee, it was not altogether surprising that the local authority, which had eliminated quite a number of cinemas as part of its redevelopment programme, decided that an art house cinema should be part of its new central library in the Wellgate shopping complex. This was the **Steps Theatre** which opened in 1979, the first new cinema venue to be opened in the city since the **Capitol** in 1956.

In the 1980s, home video recorders became so popular that the major studios unsuccessfully sought to ban them in America as a breaking of copyright. In the studios horror films were produced in greater numbers and violence was more explicit. Blockbuster films became a significant part of the entertainment offered in the cinemas. Many were sequels to previously successful films such as *Star Wars*, *Indiana Jones* and *Jaws*. And at the very end of the decade *Batman* was very successful, breaking all box office records.

But in spite of all the film industry's efforts cinema attendances kept falling and reached the low point of 54 million in 1984. Things got so bad that the government of the day abolished the Eady tax on film exhibition that had been in force since 1950. Only coincidentally film attendances began to rise in the mid 1980s, and by 1990 they were up to 97 million. But the revival was too little and too late for the **Plaza** which closed in1975, and the **Victoria** which closed in 1990.

The 1990s were a period of great technical change. Digital films arrived and brought with them computer generated images, popularly known as CGI. This development, in the words of film historian Mark Cousins, meant that "any conceivable image could be rendered in photographic reality". CGI special effects were central to the success of such films as *Jurassic Park* and *Titanic*. Animated films for family audiences were again popular, and in the middle of the decade the animated *Toy Story* was the world's first completely CGI film to be made. In 1999 Digital cinemas began to open around the world. Multiplex cinemas, which had began to be developed in the 1980s, first appeared in Dundee in 1993 when the 2,500 seater multi screen **Odeon** was opened in the Stack Leisure Park in Lochee.

Other technical developments such as the appearance of home DVD equipment in 1997 were not propitious to cinema-going, but, over the decade, UK cinema audiences continued to rise, reaching 142 million by the millennium. Nevertheless, in 1998 the **ABC** in the Seagate closed down, due in part to the competition posed by the new multiscreen that had opened at the Stack Leisure Park.

At the end of the century two new cinemas appeared in Dundee. The first was the 9 screen **UGC/Cineworld** multi screen at Camperdown which opened in 1999 and the second the 2 screen art house cinema in the **Dundee Contemporary Arts (DCA)** complex in the Nethergate which opened in the same year. The latter was not a net addition as the City Council closed the **Steps Cinema** in anticipation of the opening of the **DCA**.

It was fitting that the City Council and the University, both of which had been the agents for the demolition of so many cinemas, were involved in the creation of the **DCA**. Indeed it is more than likely that **DCA** could not have been successful without a growing population of university students and staff in the city.

2001 saw the third new cinema to be built in this period - the 10 screen multiplex **Odeon** in Douglasfield.

Since the turn of the century probably the most notable development was the re-emergence of 3D films. As in the early 1900s, the 1930s and the 1950s 3D films were initially greeted with great enthusiasm. Whether this will be sustained, or fails like earlier attempts, remains in to be seen.

The twenty first century has seen further developments designed to emulate the cinema going experience in the home. In particular larger and larger TVs, some big enough to dominate most living spaces, have become available, along with cinema type seats and stereophonic sound. This has been accompanied by a growth in free-to-view channels that show films. Digital filming has become commonplace and most computers have some sort of programme which allows the making of home movies, or something more professional, if this your aim.

In the cinemas the most remarkable feature was the amazingly successful return of the family film. This had two major strands - the Harry Potter set of films that began to be released from 2001 on, and the creatively animated pictures released by Pixar.

The net result is that audiences have plateaued at around 160 million, cinema receipts are up, and watching movies seems as popular as ever.

Nostalgia, and a growing interest in local and social history, has resulted in a series of television programmes built around films taken by early film makers.

At the same time a happy combination of increased appreciation of cinema architecture, and a desire to still watch films in cinemas has led to the restoration and reopening of some of Britain's smaller early movie houses. There has also been an increase in public interest in early cinema. Restoration of old prints of films from the 1920s and 1930s has revealed a level of wit and sophistication far more widespread than previously thought.

Courses on film studies have introduced new and younger audiences to merits of early films. Indeed one of the successful initiatives of Dundee University in the first decade of the twenty-first century has been a series of illustrated lectures given by Matthew Jarron on all aspects of the history of film.

Above all Dundee has been extremely fortunate to have the cinema at **DCA**. Although the **Steps Theatre** was vital in providing a venue for a wide range of films during the 1970s and 1980s, the advent of **DCA** with its two screens was a step change. Great credit has to given to Thomas Gerstenmeyer who was in charge of the cinema when it first opened. His creative approach to programming and his arranging of personal appearances in **DCA** of directors and stars from all over Europe was exemplary. And we are doubly fortunate that this approach has been continued and further developed by his successor Alice Black.

Sitting on the Sofa -Going to the Multi Screen

In the 21st century, seeing films is quite a different experience to that of going to the movies in the age of talkies.

The easiest way to see films is on television at home. On an average day there are more than 30 films screened on free-to-view channels, and well over 150 or

more on pay to view channels. The movie watcher probably finds out what is on from a daily list in a newspaper, or from the web, which he may well access from a mobile phone. Viewing is often interrupted by events in and around the home, and films are seen for the most part in a fully lit room that reduces their impact when compared to viewing them in a cinema.

There is a certain irony, that in 2012, a house bound movie viewer may well be using 21st century technology to watch *The Artist*, a silent film. Even more ironic is that, just as early films were interrupted by breaks to allow for reels to be changed, so his viewing is interrupted in much the same way to accommodate commercial breaks.

If the movie-goer does decide to go out to the cinema in Dundee, there are now two options - the multi-screens and the art house cinema. Newspaper adverts are no longer the way you decide what to see, as the only significant advertising is on the internet.

The multi-screens such as **Cineworld** and the **Odeon** tend to be situated in large and somewhat anonymous buildings located in the suburbs. Generous car parking is available, indeed it is hard to reach most multi-screen cinemas without a car.

The movie-goer enters a multiscreen cinema by way of a large foyer giving access to at least 5 screens and possibly as many as ten. The style is modern and anonymous, but the fug of cigarette smoke, which so characterised cinema going in earlier times, is thankfully not there. What is there is the smell of popcorn, which seems to be everywhere. The most eye-catching thing is the brightly lite sweet counter. There will be at least one cashier to sell you a ticket and one usher to take it. He or she will point you in the direction of the appropriate screening rooms but will not conduct you there. The screening room rarely have names, only numbers. There are very few staff given the enormous size of the buildings, and one finds a seat without the help of an usherette.

The spaces in which the films are screened are all rather bland although all have a steep rake, ensuring that tall men or ladies with large hairdos do not interfere with your view of the film. One noticeable feature is the volume of sound. This is at its greatest in the trailers and adverts which proceed the single main feature. You really do feel that if you had a hat it would be blown off. Although not quite so loud, the sound track for all films is significantly louder than would have been the case in the 1950s and 1960s.

Going to Dundee's only art house cinema, the **DCA**, is quite a different experience. The newspaper and the internet can be used to find out what is going on but the printed programme is made freely available to patrons and distributed around the town providing not only a list of what is on, but also write ups of the films. The cinema might show one film at set times throughout the day but will more likely show separate performances of two or more films during the day. If you are old, young, a movie buff, an enthusiast for opera or drama, or have a small child, you will find that special performances have been put on for you.

DCA Cinema

The immediate impression on entering **DCA** is of arriving at a busy meeting place to which the cinemas are an annex. The cinemas are tucked away in a corner and have an intimate air. As the common exit from the cinemas is located alongside the café/bar/restaurant, one is encouraged to linger afterwards. In a way, it is a return to the old concept of the community cinema but, writ large and, perhaps, focussed on a somewhat tighter community which revolves around the universities in Dundee.

8

The Cinemas of Dundee

Introduction

This section takes a somewhat broader than usual definition of what is a cinema, as it includes all those locations and buildings where there have known to been exhibitions of moving pictures available to the paying public. There are some locations where the showing of moving pictures was a one-off event. These have been placed at the end of the list.

The classifying of cinemas in Dundee is difficult as nearly all of them have changed their name at some time or another and some early cinemas did not even have a name. For that reason, this section deals with the cinemas in order of address which is always a constant. The address generally refers to the street in which the entrance was found.

1. The Pavilion Picture Theatre, The Palladium Picture House, The New Palladium, The Rex - 67/69 Alexander Street

The Pavilion Picture Theatre was located in Alexander Street at its junction with Carnegie Street and opened in 1913. It was built by the Pennycooks in 1912, as an 830-seater cinema with standing room for another twenty patrons. John Pennycook and his son Roger ran the cinema.

After upgrading in 1920, it was known as the Palladium Picture House. Locally it was known as 'The Plad' or 'The Peek'.

In January 1919, it was purchased by Hyman Cohen and renamed as the Palladium. At the start of the year the Palladium was showing *The Secret Game* which featured a Japanese star, Sessue Hayakawa, together with a programme of comedies, serials and a newsreel.

Hyman Cohen sold it to J. B. Milne in 1928 who renamed the cinema The New Palladium. Milne installed up to the minute sound equipment. In 1951 he refurbished and renamed the cinema after his Labrador dog Rex.

It closed in 1963 and the Alexander Street multi-storey flats that subsequently occupied the site have themselves been demolished.

2. Henderson's Booth/Noble's Picture Palace - Anderson's Lane, Lochee

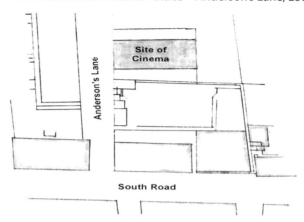

A temporary theatre was established on this site in October 1883 by a Mrs Duncan. From 1899 to 1910 this was a cinema booth used as a base by Arthur Henderson. In 1911 it was supplanted by a very basic cinema operated and owned by John Noble, although he described it as a Cinematograph Theatre. This was called Noble's Picture Palace. It was listed in the Dundee Directory for 1911-12 and was a basic building consisting of a canvas roof and wooden sides. Outside an organ played to attract customers. It closed around 1912.

3. The Picture House, The Royal Picture House - 22/7, Arthurstone Terrace

This 900 seat cinema was built by Edwards and Fraser, the architects being MacLaren, Soutar & Salmond. Joe Bell bought the Picture House in Arthurstone Terrace and carried out alterations in late 1916, early 1917.

Bell presented a mixture of films and variety shows and employed a 6 or 7 piece orchestra to accompany silent films. Further upgrading took place in 1927 to accommodate sound. In 1931, Bell sold the cinema back to Edwards and Fraser who employed architects Allen & Frisken to carry out alteration works. It then became The Royal Picture House. After World War 2 the Royal was managed by Bob Nicholson, to whom Mr Fraser bequeathed the cinema after his death.

The Royal was acquired by the Prain Brothers of Blairgowrie in October 1953, after which it continued to operate as a cinema until 1961. It then became a bingo hall and was acquired by new owners who, in 1986, turned it into a Top Rank Bingo Hall. It subsequently became a furniture depository.

4. Empress Playhouse, The Broadway Theatre - Arthurstone Terrace

On 25th November 1913 John Hagan was given a building warrant to construct a Picture House at the corner of Erskine Street and Arthurstone Terrace. In 1928 Joseph Bell bought this tin-roofed theatre with straight wooden benches. It opened in June of that year as The Empress Playhouse.

Bell sold the cinema in 1932 for £2,500 to Mrs Shand (later Mrs G White). It was then completely redesigned by architects Allan & Frisken, and rebuilt with a dropped ceiling and tip-up seats to become The Broadway Theatre, with its entrance in Arthurstone Terrace.

The Broadway offered variety, cinema and pantomime. Dundee Dramatic Society also presented productions in the Broadway.

The Broadway was one of the two cinemas in Dundee reputed to have a ghost. Although apparently harmless, it was supposedly the spectre of a long dead projectionist.

As war approached, the Broadway was purchased in early 1938 by a James Currie from Perth who closed the cinema for alterations. It re-opened in August "Under New Management". Things evidently did not work out for Mr Currie and the cinema was susequently sold to J. B. Milne in December 1939, who restyled the entrance and painted the exterior.

The Broadway was adapted for Cinemascope in 1952 but closed as a cinema in 1963 when it was converted into a Bingo Hall. It lay derelict for many years until its demolition in January 1991.

5. The Star Electric Theatre, Star Cinema Theatre - Balgay Street Lochee

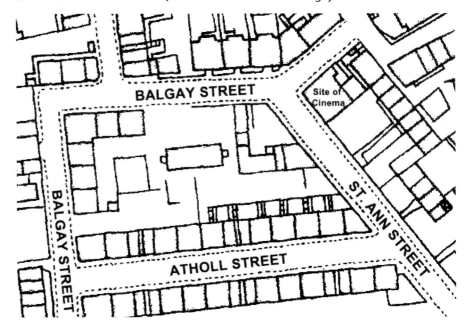

The Star Electric Theatre was built in 1911 by the McNair brothers in Balgay Street, Lochee. It stood at the junction of St Ann Street and Balgay Street. It was one of the early cinemas in this district and had a cinder floor.

John C. Noble (1887-1942), a pioneer of cinemas in Lochee, operated the cinema from 1915 under the name of the Star Cinema Theatre. The cinema closed in 1918.

The construction of the Lochee By-pass in the 1970s swept away the whole area containing the site of the cinema.

6. The Kinnaird Hall, The Kinnaird Picture House, The Kinnaird - 6 Bank Street

The Public Hall and Corn Exchange was designed by Charles Edward and built in Bank Street on land donated by Lord Kinnaird. It opened in 1858 but was not a success, closing only seven years later. Shortly afterwards, it re-opened as the Kinnaird Hall. It soon became the major entertainment venue in the city, and was used for a wide variety of uses including public meetings, concerts and lectures.

During the late nineteenth century there was a craze for roller skating in America and Great Britain. Such was the demand, a number of buildings were erected to accommodate this activity. Some entrepreneurs took the road of using existing buildings for this latest fad and the Kinnaird was no exception. It was used as a roller skating rink during the 1890s.

On 8th January 1897 moving pictures were shown at the Kinnaird as part of a Hamilton's Diorama Show. On 3rd September 1897, Walker & Company were showing "A Cinematograph Exhibition". The Courier reported that "The pictures of war were almost too realistic. One of the most outstanding and effective pictures was that showing the effects of a shell during the Graeco-Turkish War".

Thereafter moving pictures were shown on a regular basis at the Kinnaird. Notably in January 1903 it screened Melies' *A Trip to the Moon*, the pioneering French science fiction film, only months after it had been first shown in France.

In 1906 the Kinnaird was advertised an American film show:

> Every evening at 8pm; Matinees Wednesday and Saturday at 3pm
> ENORMOUS SUCCESS OF THE GREAT USA ANIMATED PICTURE Coy
> The latest and most up to date Photos in the World

Seats ranged from 2/- in the front stalls to the Balcony at 6d. The same 6d also allowed one to stand in the standing area and watch the show.

Around 1911 William Hamilton decided to settle in Dundee. His son, Victor, together with his brother, entered the cinema trade in Dundee in 1919. He secured a lease of the Kinnaird Hall and operated it as The Kinnaird Cinema with a capacity of 1,268 seats and room for 74 standing. He installed two Gaumont projectors in a concrete cinema projection box and a new winding room. The show on the opening night in 1919 consisted of *Little Miss Hoover*, *Daughter of the West*, a Gaumont Graphic newsreel and "vocal interludes".

His first year was so successful that Hamilton wanted to buy the Kinnaird outright. The owners had other ideas and put the building up for public roup. The first bid - for £15,000 was from A. E. Pickard a Glasgow cinema owner. However, Victor Hamilton won the day with a bid of £21,500.

Victor Hamilton

In 1921, the Kinnaird featured *Way Down East* which was the first film in Dundee to show for more than a week. Throughout the 1920s silent films shown at the Kinnaird were often accompanied by personal appearances. Thus when *Nanook of the North* was shown, two Eskimos were hired to appear on stage as an added attraction. There was also a 9 piece orchestra, led by Adam Patterson, who accompanied the films.

In 1928/9, Hamilton responded to the introduction of talkies by re-equipping the cinema. He also altered the hall to increase the seating capacity to 1,476 plus 70 standing.

The re-opening of the cinema for talkies was given significant coverage in the local press but the first talking picture shown at the Kinnaird was a great flop. Entitled *The Cohens and the Kellys in Atlantic City*, it featured actors with American accents so strong that they could not be understood by Dundonians. However, the following screening of *Broadway Melody* was a smash hit, and when *The Gold Rush* was shown, starring Charlie Chaplin, the queues stretched out of Bank Street and along Reform Street.

At the height of cinema going in Dundee, it could be difficult to get a seat in The Kinnaird in the evening. At one Gracie Fields picture, the waiting crowd smashed a glass door and forced their way in. For the next hour or so staff had to check if patrons had paid or not! When Laurel and Hardy appeared in *Bonnie Scotland*, there were 1,500 people inside and an estimated 500 outside!

The Kinnaird was bought by J. B. Milne in August 1944 who set up a separate company - the Kinnaird Picture House (Dundee) Ltd - to run the business. In November 1954, the Kinnaird was the first cinema in Dundee to show a CinemaScope film - *Three Coins in a Fountain*. It continued as a cinema until June 1962 when it went over to full time Bingo. It was badly damaged by fire on 2nd January 1966 and was demolished in 1969 to accommodate the Overgate shopping mall.

Interior of The Kinnaird

7. Booth, The Queen's Cinema - 15, Bellfield Street

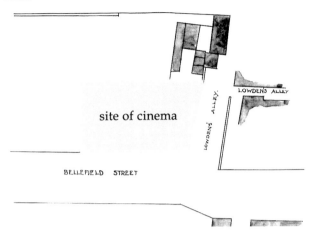

CINEMA THEATRE AT BELLEFIELD STREET
FOR ARTHUR HENDERSON ESQ.
BLOCK PLAN.

LOWDENS ALLEY

LOWDENS' ALLEY

site of cinema

BELLEFIELD STREET

Arthur Henderson showed short, silent, films in the 1890s in a canvas booth in a quarry in Bellfield Street on the site of the present St Joseph's Primary School. In 1974, Mrs McLennan remembered a piano being played to accompany the films, and that seating was on forms on an earthen floor. "Outside the cinema (were) mechanical painted figures which played cymbals. The figures were worked by a donkey engine".

In 1975, Mr Henry Skelly recalled that his job as a youth was drawing water for the traction engine that powered the dynamos which in turn provided electricity, both to the mechanical figures and to the booth.

In 1914, Henderson built the Queen's Cinema on the site of the former booth and carried out improvements to the cinema in 1916. It closed in 1928 and was susequently demolished to make way for the new St. Joseph's RC Primary School

8. The Alhambra, The State Cinema - 12, Bellfield Street

Arthur Henderson commissioned and built the Alhambra on the west side of Bellfield Street, diagonally opposite the now demolished Queen's Cinema. The Alhambra opened in 1929 with seating for 1,039 people.

This building was designed by Frank Thomson, the son of the famed city architect and engineer. Arthur Henderson, who always was interested in the theatre, decided to embark on a season of live theatre shows in 1937. These extended until July 1939. However, this was an unsuccessful attempt to bring live theatre to Dundee.

The Pennycook chain of cinemas acquired the Alhambra Theatre in 1940 and renamed it as the State Cinema. It was sold to the J. B. Milne chain in 1959, who in turn sold it to the City Council in 1968. It closed as a cinema in July 1965 after showing Garbo classics for a fortnight. It reopened as a civic theatre on 29th November 1969, renamed as the Whitehall Theatre. Until recently, it was owned locally and operated by the Whitehall Theatre Trust.

9. Edward's Picture Palace, The Tivoli Theatre, The Tivoli - 20, Bonnybank Road

This building was originally built in 1910 by Mr James Robertson. However, by 22nd February 1911, the City Council official register of cinematographic exhibitors included the premises as 'Edward's Picture Palace', a 1,000 seater cinema owned by Mr W. S. Edwards. His premises were then renamed as the Tivoli Theatre in 1913.

A shortage of films available during the First World War created a problem for the Tivoli and it was for a while run as a Music Hall, but it soon reverted to being a cinema. It operated in this mode until, in 1924, it was severely damaged by fire. The extent of the damage can be estimated when it is considered that it required a £15,000 renovation to bring it back into operation, a tidy sum in those days.

His son, James Lindsay Edwards took over the business on the death of his father, who died in 1947 and in January 1953 carried alterations and additions to the cinema.

In 1957, the widowed Mrs Edwards, sold the cinema to Mr Bill Smith who had been its chief projectionist since 1936 having started in the cinema industry as a spool boy at The Regent in Main Street. When the slump in cinema attendance began in the 1950s, he introduced quality continental films, particularly after La Scala stopped showing programmes for the Dundee Film Society in 1963. As these were not quite as popular as hoped, the Tivoli put on seamier Continental X certificate films along with them.

In 1964, the Tivoli became only the second cinema in Britain to open a cocktail bar on its premises. In 1968, it became the only Scottish cinema prepared and permitted to show *Ulysses*. This attracted film-goers from all over Scotland, some arriving in bus parties.

Alex Braid recalled that "The Tivoli was the only cinema that I ever encountered that did not have dimmable lights in its auditorium. There was always a moment of total blackness before the start and at the end of the film".

Competition for customers was fierce in the declining cinema market. In order to give something different, Bill Smith and his wife Christina (known as Nina) also sold sandwiches and served coffee to customers in their seats. This often resulted in an unexpected accompaniment of chinking crockery to the film of the day.

While attendances at the Tivoli held up better than many other cinemas the number of patrons still decreased. For a while, a weekly Chinese film club ran in the cinema and Asian films were shown every month or so.

The Tivoli closed it's doors for the last time on Saturday, 27th August 1977. It was taken over by the Dundee Health Services Social and Recreational Club. Today, it houses a billiards and snooker club.

10. UGC/Cineworld - Camperdown Leisure Park

This multi screen cinema complex opened in September 1999 as part of an entertainment complex that includes a skating rink. The cinema has 9 screens that can house 1850 patrons and has access to extensive parking. The company that originally owned the cinema was a French company, Union Generale Cinematographique, (UGC), which had set up a subsidiary company in the United Kingdom.

In October 1999, UGC purchased the Branson Cinema group. However in December 2004, it sold out to the Blackstone group and thereafter traded under the name Cineworld.

11. The Caird Hall, The Caird Cinema - City Square

William Hamilton's Diorama during the 1920s regularly appeared at Christmas and the New Year. He often included silent films as part of the programmes shown. In order to show the films, an extending screen was stretched across the Organ Gallery. By the end of 1930, Hamilton had handed the business over to his sons who gave up on the Diorama were showed films like this;-

> Visit HAMILTON BROS Colossal Comedy Season
> BUSTER KEATON in one large scream 'THE CAMERAMAN
> SYD CHAPLIN in CHARLIES AUNT

In the early 1930s, the Caird Hall in the City Square showed films intermittently but in 1938 new sound equipment was installed. This obviously worried the Dundee Branch of the Cinematograph Exhibitors Association who commented in the Courier of April 11 1938: "we are watching the Caird Hall talkies proposal with some interest to see how it develops". Pennycook Cinemas Ltd. operated cinema shows here during World War 2.

It was known as The Caird when a cinema and was included in a list of 25 Dundee cinemas in the Evening Telegraph dated 21st February 1946, when it showed films on Saturdays from 1.30pm.

In 1981 a cinema-goer recalled that "you could always be sure of a seat in the Caird. Another reason for liking it was that the seats were spaced farther apart and you could always stretch out your legs".

A further testament to the Caird came from Bill Ramsay who in 1982 recalled that "What made the Caird so good was that it had a fairly big screen, bigger than any other of the cinemas in town and the projector had a tremendous throw".

12. The YMCA Hall - 10, Constitution Road

It is not known exactly when the YMCA started screening film shows but one of the first screenings was on 15th October 1897 when a show of films was given by Peter Feathers.

Thereafter films were shown there on an occasional basis. On 2nd January 1901 it advertised that in the large Hall it would be showing "Great Cinematograph Entertainment - Tickets 6d and 3d at Door".

It first applied for a cinema licence on 31st August 1910 when its application was deferred, probably to allow further inspection of the premises. It was granted its licence on 27th September of the same year. Thereafter it showed films on an intermittent basis. Screenings were usually associated with particular events.

On 25th March 1930, it gave a showing of the film *Deferred Payment*. This was the last known film performance held at the YMCA as later that year its exhibiting licence was withdrawn as the premises were not considered to be sufficiently safe.

13. The King's Theatre & Hippodrome, The King's Theatre Cinema, The Gaumont, The Odeon - 27 Cowgate

The King's & Hippodrome theatre was designed by Frank Thomson and opened on 15th March 1909. Its very large stage enabled the presentation of not only plays but operettas, variety shows and musicals. From its start, it showed moving pictures as part of its shows. On 2nd April 1909 it gave a performance of animated pictures on its "Kingoscope". The King's was one of the establishments that were granted a Cinematograph licence on 25th February 1910.

With the closure of Her Majesty's Theatre in 1919, the King's became the main theatre in Dundee. In 1928, it became a cinema and was renamed the King's Theatre Cinema with a seated capacity of 1,450 and room for 288 paying customers.

The King's was known at that time for the size of its orchestra which comprised 16-18 players under the direction of Ernest McPherson. Guy Hughes (violin), who was the leader later became its director.

There was also an organ in the King's. This was a 2-manual 6-unit Wurlitzer (Style 165) and was installed in 1928. Its installation involved the conversion of the old theatre boxes, one on each side, to form organ chambers. The organ, which was on a lift, survived until 1960.

The King's tried to cater for all kinds of customers. It had a café and soda fountain which enabled cinema goers to have a meal prior to seeing the show. During World War Two, Garrison Theatre Shows were featured on Sunday night. The King's for many years, hosted a King's Club for children on Saturday mornings. At one stage this was so popular that there were several houses denoted by the colours red, blue, and green.

The Gaumont British chain acquired the King's in May 1950 from the Provincial Cinematograph Company and promptly renamed it the Gaumont. Major structural alterations took place in the summer of 1961 including the disappearance of the large stage and "the gods" or upper circle where even in the 1950s you could see the show for 1/6d (7½p).

Gaumont British (GB) continued the Saturday club for children. Particularly liked was the fact that on your birthday you got a card from Gaumont entitling you to a free entry and a free drink of lemonade.

The King's was altered yet again and was re-opened in 1973 as a super cinema at which time it was renamed the Odeon. It survived as a cinema for a further eight years until 1981, after which it housed The County Social Club, which closed for business in 1994.

The building was then bought by Leicester-based First Leisure Corporation and renamed in 1998 as Brannigan's Entertainment Bar. It then became the 'Déjà Vu' night-club. The King's Theatre Group has since sought funding to restore the King's to its original glory and bring it back into use as a theatre.

14. The Odeon - Douglas Road

The Odeon opened in November 2001 as part of an out-of-centre entertainment complex. It has 10 separate screens and a seating capacity of 2,500.There is extensive parking. At the time of its construction, the Odeon name was owned by the Rank group, but since that time there have been a whole chain of buyouts and mergers. However, the Odeon chain remains the largest in Europe and the UK.

15. The Olympia Palace/Olympia Skating Rink - 28, East Dock Street

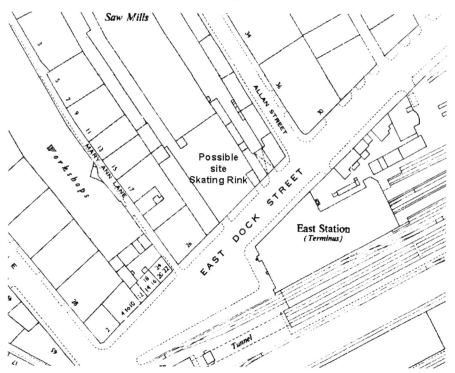

The Olympia seems to have been opened to cater for what proved to be the short lived craze for roller skating.

It is not known when films were shown at these premises but on 1st January 1910 a building warrant was issued to Cruikshanks and Co for an 'addition to the cinematograph box' at the Olympia Skating Rink. It therefore seems likely that there had been pictures shown at this location before this date. In March 1910 a Cinematograph Licence was issued by the City Council to John Lavesque Adams.

There is no known advertising evidence that these premises were ever used for public film performances although pictures may have been projected upon a screen or wall as an accompaniment to skating. Shows may have been publicised at the rink, or by means of handbills, which was quite a common method at the time.

It was open until 1912 at the least, and it may be significant that its Managing Director was a D. Oppenheim who, in 1910, was issued with a Cinematograph licence in respect of a temporary cinema at 62, Logie Street (later the site of the Astoria).

16. The Forest Park Cinema - Forest Park Road

The Forest Park Cinema stood in Forest Park Rd on its corner with Forest Park Place. It had seating capacity of 1264 seats and space for another 10 standing customers. It was built by Charles Gray and opened on Hogmanay 1928. For the Gala opening there was 6 piece band and the opening film was *Two Little Drummer Boys* starring Wee Georgie Wood.

The Forest Park was one of the out-of-centre cinemas in Dundee and showed up to three changes of programme each week. It had a 6-piece orchestra that played on Mondays, Wednesdays and Saturdays and a 10-piece band that played on Tuesdays, Thursdays and Fridays.

On 5th November 1940, a bomb dropped by a German Luftwaffe plane hit the nearby electricity sub-station. This blacked out the cinema and the surrounding area. The film being shown, when the cinema was plunged into darkness, was *The Ghost Comes Home*. The cinema, although damaged, withstood the blast and no one inside was hurt.

It was upgraded in 1949 by Grays Cinemas Ltd and, in 1953, a panoramic screen was installed which "was also suitable for three dimensional films."

Vera Winslow recalls "I remember going with my uncle Jim on Tuesday nights to Forest Park cinema to see the cowboy movies. My uncle always said 'we can't go in the front row, we'll just get the dust from the horse's hooves in our eyes'

The 'Forrie' finally closed in June 1967, became a carpet salesroom and then an athletic organisation's clubrooms. There is now housing on the site.

17. Broughty Ferry Picture House, Reres Cinema - 44 Gray Street, Broughty Ferry

Local Councillor George Greig built the Broughty Ferry Picture House which opened in 1916. His wife ran the business and employed May Crabbe as a pianist to accompany films in the silent era.

In 1953, it became the Reres Cinema although locally it was always 'the Broughty'. Bob Stewart recalled, "It was always the second choice cinema in Broughty Ferry and was never full. It ran a Saturday morning session for kids and, unusually, had no curtain across the screen".

It survived until its closure in 1963.

The cinema front remains but it now houses a number of commercial premises.

18. The Rialto Cinema - 1 Gray's Lane, Lochee

Arthur Binnall built the Rialto, which had a capacity of 1,175 and opened in October 1927 with a showing of a western entitled *The Burning Cross*.

It was designed with a Mexican themed exterior and a Chinese Garden themed interior. In its exotic interior it had a projection box in the shape of a Chinese face with lights shining out of the eyes and a barrel vaulted ceiling. The Rialto was, in the terms of the day 'an atmospheric'. To provide further atmosphere, the Rialto had a six piece orchestra which sat on a garden bridge and provided a backing for its silent pictures.

The Rialto was one of three Dundee cinemas to show simultaneously the first talking pictures in the city on the 25th March 1929. According to a contemporary account eight 10 minute short films were shown, including Armistice Day 1928, the Victoria Troupe of Dancers, a Dickens sketch, a humorous sketch and a cartoon.

A few months later on 25th June 1929, the first feature talking film *Lucky Boy* starring George Jessell was shown in the same three cinemas, in the week beginning 1st July 1929.

DUNDEE'S FIRST BIG TALKIE PRODUCTION
The film that is breaking all House Records in America
George Jessel (The Original Jazz Singer) in
LUCKY BOY

The greatest singing and talking full-length masterpiece
Showing all next week at
CINERAMA   ROYALTY KINEMA   RIALTO
The real Talkies are here! We lead again!

However, on the 1st November 1930, over a year later, it was still showing a mix of talking and silent films as when it advertised:-

---

Midnight Daddies
The first Mack Sennett All Talking and Musical Gloom Chaser
Also The Tigers Son (silent)

It was acquired by Charles Gray in 1949 and operated as a cinema until 1962 when it converted to Bingo. It is now derelict.

19 The Hippodrome, The New Hippodrome, The Princess - 160, Hawkhill

The Hippodrome was built by A. E. Binnell and opened in 1911 as one of the first purpose built cinemas in the city. It was renamed some time after as the New Hippodrome with 1,000 seats, mostly on wooden forms, and with prices set at 1d, 2d and 4d.

Bill Illingworth was the manager from 1910. He recalled that "there was keen rivalry between the Hippodrome and the Magnet in nearby Well Road. To attract customers, especially children, one would offer free bars of chocolate and oranges, whilst the other gave out sticks of rock and postcards".

In 1918 it was sold to D. W. McIntosh who reopened the cinema in 1919 as The Princess. McIntosh, as were many at the time, was a member of the Temperance movement. McIntosh allegedly said that he bought the cinema to offer Dundonians a pleasant alternative to drink! However temperance was not everyone's cup of tea and even under McIntosh's ownership drunken brawls occurred from time to time.

This led the employment of special staff to control the miscreants. Even so, the police had sometimes to be called in to deal with trouble in the cinema caused by drunken patrons.

In the early years of its life cine-variety was presented on its stage. When it became a 'talkie' on the 10th March 1931, the seating capacity was reduced to 650 for fire safety reasons, but only after considerable discussion with Dundee Council.

Miss Minnie McIntosh, who ran the cinema after her father's death in 1928, became a very prominent and well respected member of Dundee's cinema community. She pioneered children's cinema clubs on Saturdays from 1944 - at one time the Princess had 2,580 child members. The Princess was featured in the book 'Picture Palace' by former film censor Audrey Field who described it as "an archetypal example of the 'family' picture house".

Miss McIntosh became secretary of the Dundee branch of the Cinematograph Exhibitors Association and an active member of the national committee. She was a prominent supporter of Sir Alexander B. King in his campaign to eliminate the tax on cinema seats. Her basic instinct was always to stand up for the interests of the locally owned cinemas whenever these were threatened by the actions of the big cinema chains.

In 1959, after being made an offer by the then Queen's College (later to become the University of Dundee), Miss McIntosh finally decided to close the Princess. Almost immediately it was demolished to make way for the development of the University campus.

20. The Royal British Hotel - High Street

On the 7th October 1896, Peter Feathers gave the second public screening of moving pictures to be seen in Dundee. This took place in the Royal British Hotel in the High Street where he had hired a room. Later, Feathers who was the first to make his own films in Dundee, claimed that this was the first showing of moving pictures in the city, but this was not the case. (See the People's Palace). This was the only known showing of pictures in this location.

In October 1996, a tribute plaque commemorating his great contribution to the cinema was placed on an adjacent wall near his old shop in Bank Street.

21. The Plaza Theatre & Cinema - 103 Hilltown

Lord Provost High opened The Plaza cinema-theatre on 30th May 1928. Mr Headrick, the owner, was one of the city's most successful businessmen.

The cinema had cost between £25,000 and £30,000 to build. The architects were Messrs McLaren, Soutar and Salmond of Dundee and the builders were J. B. Hay & Co of South Tay Street. The Plaza was built on a grand scale having a seating capacity of around 1,600 seats and standing capacity for 300. The stage was very large and with a working area of 29 x 30 feet could take all kinds of theatrical events. There were seven well-appointed dressing rooms to accommodate performers backstage. There were substantial galleries and a three-console pipe organ was situated to the right of the stage. The Plaza also accommodated an orchestra when it presented opera or variety shows.

The opening programme consisted of a Mack Sennet comedy *The Old Barn* and *The Squall,* a drama set in Hungary, with Myrna Loy and Alice Joyce playing the leading parts.

Only fifteen months later the theatre was bought by Associated British Cinemas Ltd,. It was then equipped with the Western Electric System, which represented the latest developments in talkie apparatus. It re-opened on 24th September 1929 as "The Sound Cinema" but retained its name rather than being renamed as ABC.

In 1958, J. B. Milne acquired the Plaza for £30,500. Alex Braid who worked in the Plaza recalls "it was a very difficult cinema to heat. I remember having to fire up the coke boiler in the morning to get the cinema heated up for the evening shows".

After operating with cinema and bingo, it stopped showing films in September 1972. Subsequently Wharton Enterprises Ltd of Middlesborough renovated and modernised the interior closing off the balcony. It then opened as Gilly's Prize Bingo in February 1973.

Interior of the Plaza

The Plaza later closed for a period until, in April 1975, the Hynd Brothers were granted a licence to show films primarily for children. The cinema was later acquired by the City Council and after lying empty it was demolished in 1996. New housing now stands on the site of what was once one of Dundee's largest cinemas.

22. The Grand Theatre, The New Grand - 22 King Street, Broughty Ferry

Joe Bell bought the Grand Theatre in 1912. It had a corrugated iron roof which was very noisy in heavy rain, providing unwanted sound effects which drowned out the musical accompaniment to the silent action on the screen. It had basic seating that consisted of long wooden benches in the front rows where seats cost only 2d.

In 1918, Bell sold the Grand to Robert Saunders. He upgraded the dearer seats at the rear of the cinema by adding cushioning and a thin layer of velvet. Music was provided by Cecil Low to accompany the silent films shown this time.

It became the New Grand in 1931. Note the uniformed page boy outside the New Grand when in 1933 it was showing *Heroes for Sale*, an American drama and *Cuckoo in the Nest* a British comedy. By 23rd April 1934 it was owned by Mrs Shand Scott. It was taken over in February 1939 by a Stanley Gibbon. Louise Humphries then took over the running of the Grand which finally closed in 1940. It was later demolished and housing now stands on its former site.

23. The UNO Picturedrome, The Universal Cinema -
30. Lawrence Street, Broughty Ferry

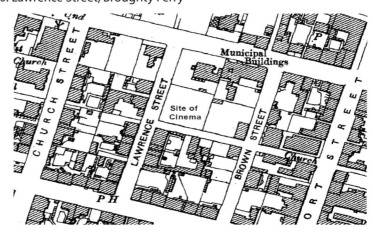

On this site, James Stewart and his brother Alexander, built a wooden-shed picture house which they operated through The Universal Cinematograph Company. The Universal or UNO was granted a cinema licence in 1913. The UNO showed films from 1913 to 1915 and was located roughly in the area of the present Marks & Spencer's car park.

Although there is no evidence of the UNO advertising in local papers a Broughty Ferry joiner recalled finding a playbill for the UNO when renovating a cottage in Broughty Ferry. Unfortunately it's whereabouts is unknown.

24. The People's Picture Palace, The Oxford Picture House, The Astoria -
60/2 Logie St, Lochee

In 1910, there was a cinematograph licence application for a "Temporary Picture Palace" on this site, the applicant being a Mr D. Oppenheimer. A permanent 900 seat cinema was built on the site in 1911 by J. J. Bennell. It was called the B & B People's Picture House and opened in 1912.

It had aspirations, as in November 1913 it screened the Italian film *Quo Vadis*, a lengthy epic, but, with attendances in mind, patrons were assured that there would be "No increase in prices".

By 1914, the cinema had changed hands once more, the new owner being Mr John Noble, in whose possession the cinema remained until 1920. Noble changed its name to the Oxford Picture House. In 1920 it was bought by the Alhambra (Leith) Co. Ltd.

The Oxford ran two shows per night of silent movies. Stage performances including local talent shows were used to fill in the gaps between films. This was necessary as there was only one projector. A Dundonian living in the USA remembered going to the Oxford in about 1924. "There was vaudeville in the programme. I had an apple which I dropped on the floor and it rolled into the orchestra pit. The picture I can't remember, of course". Accompanying the silent films was an 8 piece orchestra.

In April 1924, the cinema was put up for sale but remained vacant for some time. In November 1929, it was bought by A. E. Binnall and reconstructed to become **The Astoria**. Its opening bill comprised two feature films, *Hawks Nest* and *Vamping Venus*. It was bought by Charles Gray in 1936 who operated the cinema for the next 40 years.

Its interior must have been a little anonymous as Craig McGeochie, who clearly remembers seeing *Where Eagles Dare* at the Astoria, can recall nothing of the interior décor or layout.

It was closed in 1977, purchased by the City Council for road improvements,which never took place and demolished.

25. The Main Street Picture Palace, The Regent Picture House - 20, Main Street

In 1912, George Stewart Adams opened the Main Street Picture Palace. In 1920, it was acquired by Glasgow Film Services Ltd. On 22nd June 1920, permission was given to the Main Street Picture House Co. Ltd. by the City Council for a new building to replace the existing structure. The new building, which had 1,000 seats, became the Regent Picture House in 1922.

Around 1924, the cinema closed for a while and was acquired by Edwards & Fraser in 1927 who operated it until 1953.

The Regent was then bought by Prain Brothers, of Blairgowrie from Edwards & Fraser in October 1953. A former projectionist remembered well the all concrete projection room which "was freezing in the winter and stifling in the summer".

It closed as a cinema in 1962. Later, the building was re-opened as the Regent Bingo Hall and as one of Dundee's oldest cinema buildings was finally closed on Sunday 13th October 1991. It was demolished in 1995 and flats now stand on the site.

26. The City Picturedrome - Milnbank Road

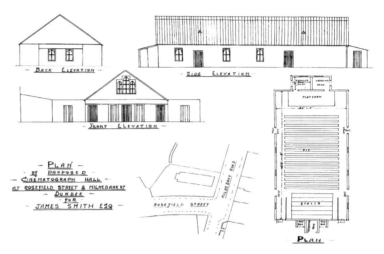

In April 1911, an application was made by James Smith to the City Council to build a cinematograph hall and, as can be seen from the drawing above, the **Picturedrome** was fairly primitive building. It opened in 1913 but only lasted about two years after which the building was occupied by a garage business.

27. The New Cinema, Stobswell Cinema Theatre The Ritz - 12 Morgan Street

In 1910 Peter Feathers commissioned the architect J Sibbald and built a cinema on the west side of Morgan Street, with 850 seats to accommodate films and variety shows. This was the New Cinema. There was a small balcony to the side of the screen to house the orchestra but there was no ceiling below the iron trusses that supported the roof.

The front page of the Dundee Courier on Thursday 17th May 1914 advertised a performance to be given at The New Cinema. 'Grand galaxy of local films. Dundee Territorials' Church Parade in Victoria Park, Boys' Brigade Inspection in Baxter Park. Masonic Church Parade. The above films specially taken by Mr Peter Feathers.'

It became The Stobswell Cinema-Theatre later in 1914. Feathers sold it on in 1931. It was taken over by Mrs George White whose husband was the owner of The Broadway Theatre in Arthurstone Terrace.

In 1931, a programme of alterations were carried out when it changed hands again. Mr and Mrs Clive Gibb became the owners, and the movie house reverted to its old name of the New Cinema.

Just before World War Two, it was sold to Thomson Pennycook. One of the oldest cinemas in the city, it was seriously damaged by fire in May 1945. Mr William Pennycook re-opened it in 1948 after alterations, with its seating capacity reduced to 665.

The J. B. Milne chain of cinemas bought it in 1959, painted the outside silver with a black plinth and rechristened it The Ritz. It became somewhat run down and Milne had some seats removed to accommodate buckets placed to catch water from the leaks in the roof.

Unusually, we have a first hand account of what the cinema was like at this time from Alex Braid. He recalls that:-

"The Ritz, Morgan Street, was the first cinema in which I worked. I have fond memories of this little cinema which was originally the Stobswell Cinema Theatre. Only J. B. Milne had the brass neck to rename such a humble little fleapit The Ritz, a name with connotations of grandeur and luxury. Neither was in evidence in this cinema. I clearly recall my disappointment when I first had sight of the building. However, I quickly overcame this and enjoyed my time there.

The Ritz had a narrow entrance with the pay box window almost in the street. One pair of double doors led into the narrow foyer with its patterned terrazzo flooring. There were two large Lyons Maid Ice Cream fridges in the foyer as there were no storage rooms in the building.

At the far end of the foyer a narrow staircase led to the miniscule manager's office on the upper level. The projection room was accessed by walking through the office and out onto an external gangway at each end of which there were two doors into the "box" as projections rooms were called.

The Ritz was equipped with two Kalee Model No 11 variable speed projectors together with Kalee Vulcan Arc lamps. These elderly machines were beautifully maintained and gleamed as we cleaned them with great care every morning. We also swept and mopped the box floor daily.

The auditorium was long and narrow. There was none of the elaborate decoration and lighting found in the great super cinemas of the thirties. The main auditorium houselights were wall mounted each side of the auditorium. There were footlights mounted at the front of the tiny stage. These illuminated the plain side opening stage drapes.

The screen was without any doubt the worst in Dundee. The proscenium was too narrow for CinemaScope and the only way films in this ratio could be screened was by dropping top masking over the upper part of the screen. This meant that Cinema Scope films were squeezed into a reduced area of the normal screen (by using special anamorphic lenses) resulting in a total loss of the visual impact these films were intended to make.

The Ritz screen had never been replaced or even resprayed. Years of rain water penetration together with cigarette smoke had combined to produce large dirty marks on parts of the screen. These were clearly visible during the lighter scenes of films.

The seats were ancient and in common with most J. B. Milne theatres, the runners down the aisles were not carpet but rubber.

Programs ran twice weekly on Mon, Tues and Wed with a change on Thur, Fri and Sat. Dundee cinemas at that time were allowed to open one Sunday in five, films on Sunday could only be screened between 6.31pm and 9.59pm. The Ritz never had Sunday shows.

Double features were still standard at that time. The Ritz was continuous daily from 5.30pm with the main film at approx 5.45pm and 9.00pm and the supporting feature at 7.15pm.

Despite all its many failings and dilapidated appearance the Ritz was a popular local cinema. There were still many regular patrons who came weekly. We often had audiences of 200 or more and sometimes the cinema almost filled it's 600+ capacity.

Like most cinemas from the golden era of film going, the Ritz had atmosphere and individuality, something lacking in the sterile and bland auditoria of the present day multiplexes.

The box office cashier had been there for years and was known to everyone who came to the Ritz. She would have a chat or gossip with regulars, can you imagine that today. I forget her name, she had married a Pole after the war and her surname was difficult to pronounce, something like Sienkiewicz.

The manager of the Ritz at that time was Charles (Chic) Coutts, a long serving J. B. Milne manager, the Chief and only projectionist was Lennie Mitchell, and I was the trainee".

In 1961, it had another fire, this time confined to the projection room and in September 1970 it was hit by fire yet again. Ironically the film scheduled to be shown that night was *The Frozen Dead*.

After J. B. Milne's death in 1968, the cinema was bought by Kingsway Entertainments Ltd of Kirkcaldy. The Ritz was closed in 1973 and demolished in 1978 to make way for modern housing.

28. La Scala - 30 Murraygate

In 1912, the Dundee Picture Theatre Company Ltd applied to the local authority for permission to build a cinema. The result was La Scala. It was designed by George Boswell of Glasgow and financed by Mr Ramsay Blair of Picture Theatre Ltd who owned a chain of over 20 cinemas.

La Scala was Dundee's first building to be constructed solely as a picture house and was opened on the 9th December 1913 by Lord Provost Urquhart. The cinema

seated 1,099. Clad in faience, its façade was topped by a tower surmounted by a golden globe. Its opening show was of a single film *Moths,* adapted from what was regarded at the time as a somewhat racy novel by Ouida.

La Scala ran continuous performances from the start and initial opening prices were 3d, 5d, 9d, and 1/-.

In May 1915, a typical programme consisted of *Saved from Destruction,* a western drama, Charlie Chaplin in *Tillie's Punctured Romance,* and a 6 part Keystone Cops film. Shortly after this, La Scala went over to double bills with three changes of programme every week. It showed continuous performances of films from 2.30 to 10.30 pm. Prices of admission were 3d, 6d and 1/-, with private boxes for four at 5/- and 7/6d.

It was altered and upgraded in March 1923 when the owners name had changed to Dundee Cinema Palace Ltd.

Denis Naulty recalled that, "Its interior decor created an atmosphere of exoticism and luxury, an aura of romance and excitement, another 'dream palace'. Unusually when you entered the auditorium, you did so by the side of the screen and walked up the side aisle with your back to the action".

The quality of the resident orchestra was used as an advertising ploy and with good cause. To accompany silent films La Scala had an 18-piece orchestra, one of the biggest in Dundee cinemas. On stage it had Routledge Bell, leader, Jimmy Deuchars (violin), brothers Rob (violin) and Dave Phin (cello), 'Birkie' Bill (Bass); John Lynch (trumpet) and Mr Irvine (trombone); Arthur Milne (clarinet), a flute player, a female pianist and Billy Wallace (drums). Bert Brown took over from Dave Phin on the cello. His pay then was £3.10s a week, playing from 2.30-4.30pm then from 6.30pm to closing. A pianist would play during his 4.30-6.30pm break.

La Scala was the last cinema to install a sound system to take the 'talking pictures' in May 1930. The cinema was sold by the Globe Trust to H. Winocour in 1941. Harry Winocour, formerly known as Hersz Winorkur, was the owner of an impressive chain of cinemas in England and Scotland.

La Scala suffered badly from not being owned by one of the large cinema chains that came to dominate the cinema industry. This meant that, although a very good cinema, it could only get second run films, which placed it at a serious competitive disadvantage. La Scala closed as a cinema on 1st May 1965 when it was acquired by F. W. Woolworth & Co Ltd for the extension of their premises in the Murraygate.

29. The People's Palace, The Picture Palace, The Savoy Picture House, The Palace Cinema ,The Palace, The Palace Theatre - 160 Nethergate

The **People's Palace**, which was designed by the architect J. Hutton, opened in January 1893. The Palace gave the first public showing of moving pictures in Dundee on 8th July 1896 when it advertised a showing of films on Paul's Animatograph. After this it showed moving pictures on a regular basis. It worth noting that, as early as October 1896, a condition was applied to the renewal of its theatre licence to the effect that 'a fireproof projection room be installed'.

Often in those days film shows consisted of short news films. Thus on 3rd November 1896 the People's Journal reported that at the People's Palace in the Nethergate, "The bill of fare presented to the many patrons this week is one of all round merit, and the large audience present last night was not slow to show its appreciation of the various items submitted. The item that attracts most attention is Paul's 'theatrograph', or animated pictures. Among the many lifelike pictures shown last night were *Bathing at Trouville, Serpentine Dance, Garden scene, Arrival of express train at Calais,* and *Henley Regatta*. Most interest was taken in the presentations of *The Czar and his suite passing through Paris*, and *Persimmon winning the derby*".

In June 1898 the Courier reported that "The entertainment now open in the People's Palace is one of rare attractive merit, the dioramic pictures are artistically of high value and the series of events portrayed is of sterling interest. The marvels of the cinematograph show the rush of an express train, the fire engines of New York and the swing of the Jubilee procession".

Films had not yet won the day however, for two years later, in June 1898, Charles Poole put on a show of his Myriorama, a montage of still pictures, in this case showing scenes from the American Spanish War. Nevertheless, his show also included moving pictures under the heading "Poole's Eventograph or improved Cinematograph, several fine films, no flickering".

On 6th April 1901, the Palace had an intriguing programme advertised as:

> 'Extraordinary Attraction.
> A remarkable animated picture of a very weird incident attributed to the famous 'Stolen Anchors' picture by Gainsborough'.

After the cinemas acquisition by J. J. Bennell in 1909, it became the Picture Palace one of the 'Bright and Beautiful Pictures chain. The cinema was run on Bennell's behalf by Mr Tom Lunn and had two houses per night at 7pm and 8pm. It was adapted for theatre and variety and it was bought by Dundee Entertainments Ltd., who reopend it as The Savoy Picture House on 14th November 1918 with the following programme.

> SAVOY PICTURE HOUSE
> Continuous Performance 6.30 to 10.20. Saturdays 4.30 to 10.20.
> 'THE TOUCH OF THE CHILD' Featuring Henry Edwards and Alma Taylor.
> Monday, Tuesday, Wednesday, 11th, 12th 13th November.
> Prices of Admission:
> Balcony 3d. Front Stalls 5d. Centre Stalls 9d. Res. Stalls 1/3d.

After some years it closed again, only to reopen on 8th December 1924 as the Palace Cinema with 1,209 seats. Its first showing featuring Rudolph Valentino in *Blood and Sand*.

It reverted to being a theatre in 1938, as the Palace, and continued to put on variety shows until 1965. Calum Kennedy, the singer, bought it in that year, changing its name yet again, this time to The Theatre Royal. The theatre closed in 1968, after which it was only opened sporadically for amateur and professional shows. The building was destroyed by fire in the early morning of 12th October 1977 and is now demolished. Its site is now the car park to the south of the Queen's Hotel.

30. Green's Playhouse - 106 Nethergate

The Playhouse was Dundee's only super-cinema and undoubtedly the best in Dundee if not in Scotland. It was designed by John Fairweather for the Green Brothers of Glasgow.

Planning began as early as 1934 when negotiations were concluded to acquire a parcel of land from the L.M.S. Railway Co Ltd. The architect's plans were approved on 7th May 1935 and the building was constructed in just over 6 months, in spite of the first design for the tower being rejected by the City Council in October 1935.

The Playhouse was opened by Lord Provost Phin on Wednesday 4th March 1936. It had 4,126 seats and was a companion to the Playhouse in Renfield Street, Glasgow, which seated 4,300 people - these were the two largest cinemas in Europe at the

time. The Playhouse has been described as "easily Scotland's most spectaculer cinema of the 1930s and perhaps the finest of all cinemas in Scotland.

The owners were Herbert and George Green who had a cinema chain that, at its peak, controlled 24 picture houses with 40,000 cinema seats. They were also the only vertically integrated Scottish film company being involved in the making, distributing and showing of films. However, the Glasgow Playhouse had been built a decade earlier, and the Green brothers had learnt from it. They therefore designed the Dundee playhouse as a prototype for a chain of luxurious cinemas which they intended to build throughout the UK.

THE SUNSHINE CAFE, (OPEN SUNDAYS 3PM TILL IOPM.)
GREENS PLAYHOUSE, NETHERGATE, DUNDEE.

The décor was luxurious. The terrazzo floored foyer entrance led to a white marble staircase flanked by mirrors. This took the cinemagoer to the balcony and upper boxes and to the huge auditorium. This boasted a huge circular ceiling some 60 feet in diameter. Five boxes on either side of the stage were furnished with richly upholstered twin settees. The 'golden divans' took up the first 6 rows of the front balcony and were upholstered in gold velvet.

In the afternoons and evenings the Playhouse Café was a popular venue for the young as it had a dance floor and served snacks, afternoon and high teas.

The Playhouse was also suitable for live entertainment as the proscenium was 65 feet wide and the stage was 27 feet deep. For the filmgoer the original screen measured 30 feet in width by 22 feet in height. The stalls accommodated 2,570 people and the balcony with the upper boxes held another 1,556 seats.

Above the entrance in the Nethergate was a steel-framed tower of cream-tinted cement, glass and concrete, rising to a height of 87 feet. The tower feature, for which Joseph Emberton was the consultant, supported a projecting sign on which the name 'Green's Playhouse' was spelt out in illuminated neon letters with a tilted letter 'U' as the Green's advertising slogan was "We want 'U' in".

There was controversy at the time of its building and there were objections to the design of the tower led by the Dundee Chapter of the Institute of Architects in Scotland and the Dundee Arts Society. In particular, they doubted the wisdom of the Corporation passing plans for a structure overhanging the street, which would take away the prominence in the Nethergate, of St Paul's Church spire. As

mentioned above, the first design for the tower was rejected by the City Council but a subsequent design was approved.

The opening programme consisted of: *We're in the Money* with Joan Blondell, Hugh Herbert and Glenda Farrell; *Gay Lady* with Alice Brady, Douglas Montgomery and Alan Mowbray; a coloured cartoon *Merry Old Soul*; and a Paramount newsreel of topical events.

Throughout the 1940s and the 1950s, the Playhouse was considered by many to be the prime venue for picture going in Dundee. But with the advent of television, film attendances fell away in the 1960s and bingo evenings gradually replaced films. By January 1968, the Playhouse had really become a bingo hall as films were only screened on every third Sunday.

However, it was still an attractive venue and in 1970, the cinema was bought by Mecca who then ran daily bingo sessions in the Playhouse. Then, on 21st August 1995, the building was destroyed by a massive fire. It was replaced by new building on the same site which incorporated a replica of the original tower on its Nethergate frontage.

31. The Electric Theatre - 122 Nethergate

Peter Feathers opened his second Electric Theatre in 1910 in an adapted shop that stood where the Marketgait now lies. The price of admission, 6d (children 3d) included a cup of tea and a biscuitwhich were served in the tea-room downstairs with its wicker tables and chairs. The programme, as was normal at that time, was made up mainly of news films and 'shorts', such as the *Royal Visit to Dublin*, *The Investiture of the Prince of Wales*, *Elephant Racing at Perak*...

There were continuous showings from 2:30pm until 10:30pm. The screenings were also accompanied by an orchestra every afternoon!

In 1911 the business was sold to Mr I. Thomson of Aberdeen. The very next year the business was acquired by the Pennycook family.

The Pennycooks took quite a different approach to Feathers. On 29th July 1913 they were advertised:-

A GENTLER PASSION PATHEMACOLOUR In 3 parts 3,500feet

By 1915 the films were a bit racier. On 11th December, the advert in the Evening Telegraph was for:-

Sensational Drama *House of Terror* 3 reels *Ashes of Happiness* 2 reels Pathé Colours

The Electric Theatre closed in 1923 and later the premises reverted to a shop that was occupied by Smith's the jeweller. The building was eventually demolished to make way for the western leg of the inner ring road, the Marketgait.

32. Dundee Contemporary Arts - Nethergate

DCA was built as a joint initiative by the City Council, the University of Dundee and the Scottish Arts Council. It is an arts complex built within the structure of the multi-storey garage which previously operated on this site. The one fault with the design is that limitations of the previous structure have unfortunately resulted in a less than ideal rake of the floor in the two cinemas.

When it opened in 1999 the DCA complex incorporated two screens with a total of 294 seats. Since 2011 the DCA has been an all digital cinema but retains 35mm projection equipment for showing older films. In 2011, it was equipped to show 3D films. In a typical year it gives a total of around 3000 screenings of just over 300 films. There are main stream films shown but these are carefully selected and constitute less than 10% of the total programme.

From its inception its aim has been to produce a varied programme of films that includes international cinema, foreign films, classic films and historically significant films. It also makes a special effort to provide for a wide range of filmgoers and screens programmes specifically for children – the Discovery programme, the elderly – the Citizen Kane programme and the Bring a Baby programme for mothers with young children. Its Discovery programme for children includes foreign language films to break down cultural barriers. It also runs a programme of film related talks in conjunction with Creative Scotland. Special film festivals are run on a regular basis on topics as varied as Italian cinema, the French New Wave and the Sci-Fi Screen. There are regular film related talks and notably in 2011, a question and answer sessions by video with director Werner Herzog.

Silent films, sometimes with a live musical accompaniment are regularly shown and the Cinema Republic programme is composed of films nominated by the public at large, and artists and film buffs in particular.

33. The Wellington Palace, Wellington Cinema -
47 Nelson Street / 30 Wellington Street

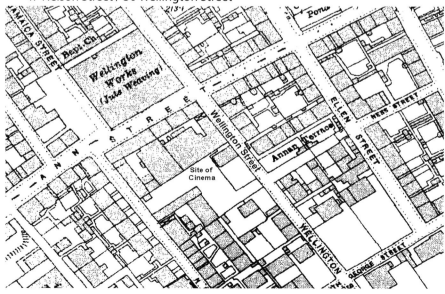

Arthur Henderson ran an early cinema show in a basic building on ground between Nelson and Wellington Streets. This forerunner of the Wellington Cinema was built in 1906. Henderson also used the trade name of 'McIndoe'- and many people called it 'McIndoe's Show'.

In 1912, Henderson decided to build permanent premises on this site and these operated as cinema under the name of the Wellington Palace. An early patron said that it had cinders or 'danders' on the floor and that he sat on a wooden bench with no back to it when he saw Edward G Robinson in *Tiger Shark* in 1932.

The cinema had 580 seats and it was renamed the Wellington Cinema by 1934 but was destroyed by fire on 23rd September 1936.

34. The Regal Cinema - 51 Queen Street, Broughty Ferry

Although there is reputed to have been a cinema called the Capitol on the adjoining site at 95 Church Street, very little is known about its existence, appearance, or duration. It is not clear whether this was the precursor to the Regal or was a totally separate enterprise.

The Regal was built by the Arbroath Cinema Company and opened by John Lyall in 1936 as a 724 seat cinema. The building had originally been a hall used by the 1st Forfarshire Artillery Volunteers. The 1936 alterations for its conversion into a cinema included the installation of a balcony. The painted mahogany panelling in the foyer and corridor areas was reputedly salvaged from Kaiser William 11's yacht, the Homeric, which had served as a Cunard cruise ship following the First World War.

In 1954, the Regal showed *The Robe*, the first CinemaScope film shown in Broughty Ferry.

The Regal was run for many years by the Humphreys sisters together with their brother. The sisters had a reputation as martinets of the first water, not being disposed to discuss their decisions on anything and insisting that staff on duty stood at all times.

By 1979, the Regal Bingo Club was operating from the Queen Street premises. It closed as a bingo club at the end of June 1991 and was sold by then the owners, Granada Leisure Group, to the West End Garage.

35. The Empire Theatre, the Empire Cinema - 62 Rosebank Street

The Empire Theatre was designed by J. McKissack and licensed to James K. Creighton in 1903. It was then the only theatre in the northern part of Dundee. Sometimes repertory companies performed in the Empire on occasions with a different play each night but right from the start the Empire showed films.

In December 1903, the Piper o' Dundee reported that "An excellent cinematograph holds the boards at the Empire this week. *Drink and Repentance* is perhaps the most interesting 'film'".

Later, in December 1903, it advertised that the following week the show would be of films by:

> The Prince Edward Animated Picture Co,
> "40 miles of Thrilling and Funny Pictures nightly.
> Greatest cinematograph in the British Isles.
> Superb varieties by Talented Artistes's".

It may be that this indicated a lease by the Prince Edward Company, for on 9th December 1905 the advert for the Empire in the Courier declared:-

> Dundee Empire loses a King, a Picture King who
> today gives his last three performances in Dundee.
> Mr Prince desires to state that he has no connection
> with any other Cinematograph entertainment whatever.
> Matinee 2.30pm Evening Performances 6.45 and 9pm

Shortly afterwards, in 1906, alterations were carried out by Frank Percival, apparently the new lessee of the Empire.

On 25 December 1909, J. J. Bennell proprietor of the 'Bright & Beautiful' Pictures chain acquired the Empire Theatre and appointed Mr R. W. Austin as its first manager.

It was never one of the top grade cinemas and when it became the Empire Cinema in 1912 a party of four could share a box for 6d! The cheapest seats were in the back pit where a series of wooden benches were nailed to a slightly sloping floor. As seats cost 2d (which was also the current price of a fish supper), they were known popularly as "the fish supper seats". It was partly destroyed by fire in 1914 but was reconstructed by Bennell.

In 1922, after the sale of the cinema to A. E. Binnall, new seats were installed as part of a programme of renovations. Five years later, in 1927 he sold the business on to the Singletons, a Glasgow company.

In the first week of July 1929, it was reported in the local press as showing Klondyke, the wonder dog starring in *The Avenging Shadow,* a melodrama of prison life. In March 1937 the Empire was sold again – this time to the Odeon chain as part of a national deal.

In its later life it was dingy to the point where it was regularly sprayed with disinfectant. At children's matinees, fun was to be had by shouting 'Move up, move up!' until the end child fell off the bench.

A second fire in 1957 led to its closure and it was demolished in 1962.

36. Her Majesty's Picture Theatre, The Majestic Cinema, The Capitol, The ABC, The Cannon - 7 Seagate

Her Majesty's Theatre & Opera House was built in 1885 by the Dundee Theatre & Opera House Company. It was designed by William Alexander and had a capacity of almost 1,300 seats. At the time, it was the most prominent building in the Seagate and staged drama, opera and musical comedy.

It is not known when Her Majesty's first began showing moving pictures but it possible that they were shown as part of a performance sometime after 1915. However, it showed them pretty well on a full time basis by 1919 and by 1925 it had been renamed Her Majesty's Picture Theatre. But in October 1929, the cinema was extensively altered and on 1st December 1930, re-opened by Lord Provost Johnston as the Majestic Cinema with seating for 1,358 and room for 119 standing.

It operated successfully as a cinema for the next eleven years but was destroyed by fire on 28th August 1941. This was not due to enemy action but the consequence of an accident, the tragedy being that a 16 year old boy who was on official fire-watching duty was killed in the ensuing fire.

The site remained a ruin until bought by J. B. Milne. He decided to build an up-to-date new cinema here which he named The Capitol and this opened on 6th August 1956.

However after only three years, Milne sold the Capitol to the Associated British Cinemas chain in 1959. In 1979, they (after refurbishment of the cinema), re-opened it as the ABC with two separate screens under one roof - the ABC1 seating 621 and the ABC2 seating 320.

It was later named the Cannon but had reverted to ABC when it closed in 1998. The closure was largely due to high heating costs, lack of parking and competition from the multiple-screened Odeon at the Stack Leisure Park.

In 1999 Yates Brothers Wine Lodges converted the building into two pubs which opened in November 2000.

37. The West End Cinema, Shand's Picture House, Gray's Cinema -
5 Shepherd's Loan

The West End Cinema was designed for Alexander Mitchell by Leslie Ower & Allan. It was a 722 seat cinema and was opened on Thursday, 28th November 1912 by ex-Bailie High. It showed 2 houses nightly, 7 and 9pm, with programmes changing twice weekly. The price of admission for adults ranged from 2d and 4d to 6d with children getting in at half-price.

Initially, it seems to have had some difficulties and had to close in the summer of 1913. On 9th August it advertised in the Evening Telegraph that it was to reopen on 1st August. It was located on a narrow street and on a confined site and when it advertised on the 20th of that month it added a line to its attractions to encourage cyclists to become customers.

> West End Cinema
> Mon, Tues, Wed
> 'The Fugitives', 'Final Justice'
> See the elopement by Aeroplane
> Cycles Stored

Later that year it posted a prominent advert in the papers stating that it had been improved and was now the cleanest cinema in Dundee.

It was brought by D. Shand in 1917 and, after alterations, was renamed as Shand's Picture House. It was further upgraded in 1920 by the Shands.

In 1928, the Shands became outcasts in Dundee's cinematic fraternity as the West End Cinema did not participate in a boycott of Charlie Chaplin pictures and thus got the first runs of Chaplin's films. As a consequence it attracted large crowds and had to open at 11.00am as opposed to its usual 3.00pm start.

Mr M. Kennedy recalls "I can still recall sitting beside Mr Shand who was blind, as he played the piano to the silent films. I eventually graduated to the post of Chocolate Boy and did a roaring trade at children's matinees". According to a contemporary Mrs Shand was the dynamic personality behind the all the progress the couple made at the cinema.

In 1934, the cinema was acquired by C. R. W. Gray who reopened it as Gray's Cinema. In 1940 he carried out alterations to the building which then remained open as a cinema until March 1958. It lay derelict for several years before being demolished to enable the expansion of the University of Dundee precinct.

38. The Britannia Picture House, The Salon, The Britannia, The Brit, The Regal - 39 Small's Wynd

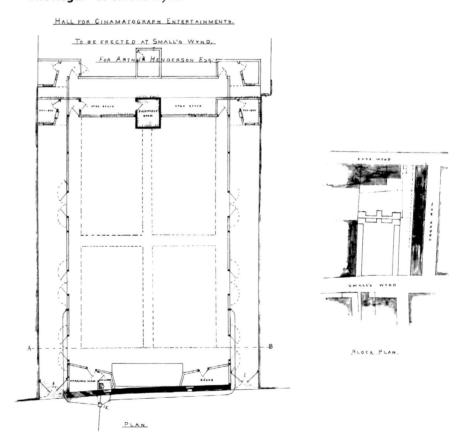

The Britannia Picture House, opened in 1911, was one of the earliest cinemas in Dundee. A smallish cinema, with some 981 seats and a steeply sloping wooden floor, it was owned by Arthur Henderson and stood roughly on the present site of

Dundee University Library. By 1923, it had been renamed the Salon but, by 1925, it had reverted to the Britannia again.

It was bought by J. B. Milne in 1936 and, after an upgrading, opened as the Brit. By 1940, it was known as the Regal but it had closed by 1963.

Mr George Camphill recalled, "The Brit had few comforts, its main attraction being the low price of admission and the type of films usually shown, mostly westerns, commonly known as 'cowsers'".

39. The Casino Picture Hall - 161, South Rd, Lochee

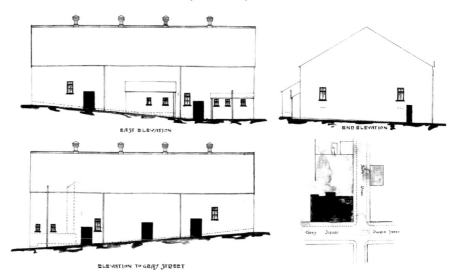

It has to be said from the start that there are some ambiguities about the history of the Casino Picture Hall. According to one account, the Casino Picture Hall was originally opened in 1910 but there is no evidence, either in the Dundee street guides or the rating and valuation records, that this was the case. Nor was any cinema licence granted for this location in the decade following the compulsory certification of cinemas in1910.

On 5th June 1922, Joe Bell was granted building permission to construct a cinema. The Casino Picture House was listed on this site in the 1925/6 street guide for Dundee. When it was listed in the 1926/7 guide, George Ayton Atkinson was given as the Lessee. However it was not until 17th May 1927 that a Cinema licence was applied for by Bell and granted by the City Council but only on a six month basis.

At the very next meeting of the Licensing Committee on the 13th June 1927, a Cinema license was granted to A. E. Binnell. But the street guide for 1927/8 gives Joe Bell as the lessee. However, Binnell held the cinema licence until 7th May 1930. In February 1930 a building warrant was granted to A. E. Binnell for alterations to the cinema but the 1930/1 street guide is the latest in which the Casino appears. The cinema is thought to have burnt down around this time.

It is known that Joe Bell was a great gambler and that from time to time he won large amounts of money. But on other occations he lost heavily. It may well be the case that Bell did have the cinema but had to sell it because of his gambling debts - but there is no concrete evidence that this was the case.

40. The Odeon - Stack Leisure Park, Lochee

In July 1991, work began on a 2,500 cinema in the Stack Leisure Park in Lochee. The Odeon opened in 1993 and was operated by Rank Cinemas. At that time it was the only multi screen cinema north of Edinburgh. Its generous parking provision was a complete contrast to the other cinemas in Dundee and thus caused major problems for them. However the Leisure park within which it was located was not successful and the Odeon only continued as a cinema until 2001.

41. The Vogue, The Odeon - 146 Strathmartine Road

There is some mystery about how a cinema came to be built on this site. In June 1935 there was an application by the Pennycooks to build a 1,500 seat cinema at the top of Strathmartine Road. But, when the application was approved in December 1935 the owner was listed as Vogue Cinemas (Glasgow) Ltd. Surprisingly, by the time that Lady Provost Mrs Phin opened the Vogue on 21st September 1936, it had become one of the cinemas of the United Cinemas Ltd chain.

Designed by McKissack & Son of Glasgow who had a track record of designing cinemas in Dundee, the Vogue was very modern cinema. For a start this cinema, unlike most others in Dundee, had a car park which could be used by its patrons. Designed to be flexible, the stage was adequate for the presentation of cine-variety, although this in some ways seemed a look back at the past. The well designed auditorium gave unobstructed views of the screen and was equipped with spacious and comfortable seating.

The opening programme included *The Littlest Rebel* starring Shirley Temple - at that time one of the most popular film stars in both Britain and America.

In March 1937, the cinema changed ownership in one of the biggest cinema deals made in Scotland. The Singleton Circuit owned by George and Ronald Singleton decided to sell ten cinemas including the Vogue and the Empire in Dundee. These were taken over by Oscar Deutsch's Odeon Theatres, an English company, and renamed as Odeons. The Odeon ran Saturday morning shows for children and was very successful, operating as a cinema for over 30 years.

In early 1973, the Odeon closed for the last time. It was then demolished, initially for a Safeways supermarket, but later a Lidl. The site is now occupied by a number of small shops.

The Odeon was very highly rated by its patrons who regarded it as a superior cinema. Audrey Shaka recalls that "The Odeon was a beautiful cinema. I still remember the sweep of the steps which took you up to the auditorium". John Scott recalled the Odeon as "The cinema you took your girlfriends to".

42. The Tay Street Cinema, The Cinerama - 57 Tay Street

The building which was later to become the Cinerama, started its life in around 1840 as a Gaelic Chapel. In 1843 it was sold to the City Council. They in turn sold it on to the Dundee Presbytery who used it as a church until 1914.

At the end of the First World War the Pennycooks rented it from the City Council. John Pennycook commissioned architects Miller & Browning, obtained permission to add a balcony and converted the former church into a cinema that they named the Tay Street Cinema.

The Tay Street Cinema had segregated areas of cheap and expensive seats and separate entrances for each area. This was not uncommon at the time.

The cinema also had a small bandstand to facilitate musical accompaniments of films. Matthew Pennycook played the saxophone and Johnny Beveridge, who was blind, played the harmonium. Beveridge had a prompter close by to give him a running commentary on the silent film so that he could relate his musical accompaniment to the action.

In 1923, it became the Cinerama and six years later John Pennycook showed the first short 'talkies' to be heard and seen in Dundee.

FIRST TIME IN THE EAST OF SCOTLAND

SEE AND HEAR THE TALKIES IN ADDITION TO USUAL
SILENT PICTURE PROGRAMME

ROYALTY   CINERAMA   RIALTO

'MIDNIGHT MADNESS'
Come and HEAR The TALKIES.
40 minutes of vocal, dancing acts, etc
Continuous 6.30 to 10.30
'The Evening Telegraph' Tuesday 26ᵗʰ March 1929

The Pennycooks were in charge of the Cinerama until in 1962 when it was closed. It was bought by the City Council for redevelopment and was demolished about 1964. The site is now part of the car park area at the top of the east side of South Tay Street.

43. The Regal - 22 Taylor St, Lochee

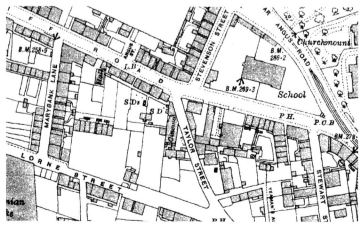

The Regal opened in 1936 on a site between Liff Road and Lorne Street. It did not last long and closed in 1939. It stood on the west side of the street. It was known locally as 'The Western' on account of the number of cowboy films it showed! It later became a dance hall and then a social club.

44. The Royal Victoria Theatre, The Gaiety Theatre, Victoria Theatre, The Vic, The Victoria - 52 Victoria Road

The Royal Victoria Theatre opened in 1842. It was used to stage plays until 1903 when music halls had become very popular. Alterations designed by W. Alexander, were approved and work started to convert it into a music hall and by 1905 it was operating as the Gaiety Theatre. On 5th December of that year, it was showing pictures as part of a variety show.

In April 1906 a review, in the Piper o' Dundee, of the current show at the Gaiety noted that: "Calder's Cinematograph is as good as ever - the lifeboat pictures being thrilling enough and the illustrated song 'Hear the Pipers Calling' capitally meets with a rousing chorus nightly". In March 1909 when the Gaiety presented Marie Lloyd the supporting programme was provided by 'The Electric Motorscope'.

It was Scotland's first twice-nightly theatre and was sold to R. C. Buchanan in 1910. He sold it to Victoria Cinema Ltd in 1915 after which it opened in 1916 as a cinema. However it continued to offer variety entertainment as well as pictures, although films became more and more predominant.

In 1919 a very varied bill of fare was advertised at the Victoria:

> 'Douglas Fairbanks in 'IN AGAIN, OUT AGAIN' (Four Reels).
> Jimmy Wilde V Joe Conn Fight.
> Fought at Stamford Bridge on Saturday, August 31st,
> under the direction of Jack Callaghan.
> Twelve Rounds of great excitement. No Padding. (Two Reels)
> ALL WEEK – CHARLIE CHAPLIN in the first of his Million-Dollar Pictures
> 'DOG'S LIFE' Three Reels of Laughter and Merriment'.

In 1933, J. B. Milne became the proprietor. He made significant changes to the interior of the building. These included the introduction of 'chummy seats' in black and gold velvet in the circle. It was believed, at the time, to be the only cinema left in Scotland with a tree-tiered auditorium. In the upper circle, the wooden seats were replaced by padded ones and from that steeply raked height there was a frighteningly vertiginous view of the redecorated cinema. A new sound system installed was the first of its kind outside London. The refurbished building was opened in 1935 as the Victoria Theatre by Lord Provost Buist.

After Milne's death in 1968, the cinema was sold to Kingsway Entertainments who in the summer of 1971, completely renovated and redecorated the building. The 'chummy seats' had gone as well as the side seats in the circle. The boxes and upper circle were also closed. It re-opened in August 1971 as an up-to-date cinema.

In January 1977 the Vic hit the headlines once again - but this time for the wrong reasons. A showing of *Jaws* led to a tremendous queue building up in Victoria Road. After the cinema was full the doors were shut, leaving around 800 outside. These people proceeded to cause a riot, necessitating a large number of police to quieten things down.

The Victoria was the last cinema in Dundee to include the British Movietone News in its programme but it ended these in May 1979. Alex Braid, who worked for J. B. Milne, recalls that the Vic was always a popular cinema.

In 1986, the Vic was rented by Border Movies and ran as a cinema for a short while. The city health officials closed the Vic after a number of structural faults were discovered in the building in May 1990. Although the Victoria had been listed as a building of historic interest, the owners, the Scottish Office and the City Council, made no objections to its demolition which took place in the summer of 1990. That was to be the end of the oldest entertainment building standing in Dundee and reputedly the second longest running cinema in Scotland.

45. The Royalty Kinema - 62/72 Watson Street

In 1919, The Edinburgh Picture House Co Ltd were given permission to erect a picture house on this site. The architects were MacLaren, Soutar & Salmond and the cinema had seating for 835 with standing space for 150.

In 1925, it was purchased by the Pennycooks. They later installed sound equipment and, on 29th March 1929, along with the Cinerama and the Rialto, showed the first talkies to be seen in the city. This was a programme of short talking films which were shown along with a number of silent films. Six months later they screened *Lucky Boy* starring George Jessel, the first all talking feature film to be seen in the city. The Royalty ran Saturday afternoon shows for children.

The Royalty Kinema was sold to the J. B. Milne chain who carried out some reconstruction in 1959. Alex Braid recalls that "the Kinema had rather exotic curtains

on the stage which featured an underwater theme. The Kinema was also notable for its very wide screen and its excessively hot projection room".

The cinema was closed round about 1965. The Royalty was purchased by the City Council for redevelopment as part of the Watson Street Comprehensive Development Area and pulled down in December 1971. It was subsequently replaced by housing.

46. The Edenbank Picture House, The Glebe Picture Theatre - 72 Watson Street

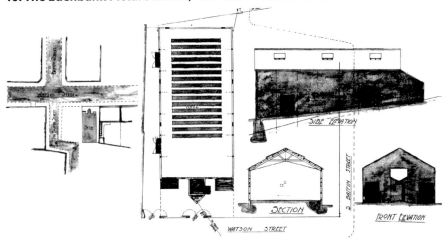

In October 1910, the City Council gave permission to John Spink to open a temporary Cinematograph Theatre in Watson Street. This was known as the Edenbank. It was an iron framed building and had ashes on the floor.

Mr Robert Miller recalled that the Edenbank was the first cinema he visited. "Proper films were not shown but snippets of silent film lasting for 5 or 10 minutes each, to a piano accompaniment. They flickered and jumped but we found them exciting. There was an area at the back of the Edenbank where there were no seats and people were allowed to stand".

The Glebe Picture House operated as a cinema until 1920 but the site had been purchased a year before this by the Edinburgh Picture House Company who incorporated it into the site of their new Royalty Kinema.

47. Queen's Hall Cinema, Queen's Cinema, Queen's Theatre - 3-5 Well Road

Arthur Henderson bought the former St Mary Magdalene's Rectory, built in 1900, at 3-5 Well Road and opened it in 1922 as The Queen's Hall Cinema with some 720 seats. From 1933-39 he ran it as The Queen's Theatre with seasons of repertory productions, notably by Herbert Mansfield's company of actors. It was showing films again in 1946 and did so until at least 1955.

The Queen's then closed as a cinema and went through a number of uses including the Queen's Ballroom, the Astoria Ballroom, the British Legion Clubrooms and latterly lecture rooms and examinations hall for Dundee University. It was finally demolished to make way for the Welcome Institute.

48. The Magnet Picture Palace - 8 Well Road, Hawkhill

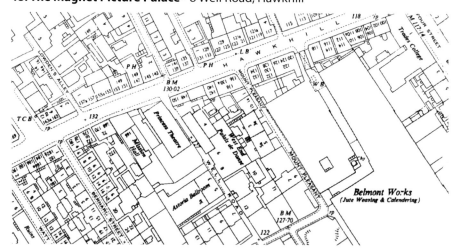

110

The Pennycook family acquired the old church hall premises in the shape of the Hope Hall and, after alterations opened it as The Magnet Picture and Variety Palace in 1912. It closed as a cinema in 1915. This building later became the West End Palais owned by Mr John Robertson. Familiarly known as 'Robbies', this was where many young Dundonians learned ballroom dancing.

49. The Steps Theatre - Wellgate Library

In 1974, the City Council approved a proposal for a regional film theatre to be located in the new Wellgate Library. The film theatre operated on Friday, Saturday and Sunday evenings with one midweek evening performance. The 250 seater cinema, with space for two wheel chairs, featured Dolby stereo, a large screen video, wide screens and the capacity to show 16mm as well as 35mm film.

The purpose of the Steps was to show new films which were not viable in commercial cinemas but which merited being screened; older films which had their place in cinema history, specialised kinds of film, independent cinema and the best commercial films.

The Gala opening of the Steps as a cinema was on Monday 23rd April 1979 when approximately 200 invited guests watched the American comedy *The Goodbye Girl* starring Richard Dreyfuss and Marsha Mason. Among those present was Lord Provost Harry Vaughan.

The first public showing took place on Friday 28th April 1979 when *Julia* starring Vanessa Redgrave and Jane Fonda played to a full house with many turned away. The Saturday and Sunday evening performances also attracted capacity audiences with queues forming across the patio entrance from Victoria Road. Cinema goers had travelled from Perth, Arbroath and Fife.

Shortly after the Steps opened, a near capacity audience of around 200 had to be evacuated when the fire alarm rang out during a screening of *Casanova,* starring Donald Sutherland. Luckily, it proved to be a false alarm and 15 minutes later the audience trooped back in to enjoy the rest of the film.

In October 1979, the Steps had a visit from *Julia* director Fred Zinneman, who spoke after the screening of the film about his favourite directors and the film industry in general.

The Steps' 16mm film projector proved essential for the very popular Archive Film Nights produced by co-operation between the Steps and Janet McBain of the Scottish Film Archive. In April 1985, hordes of film fans were turned away when Janet's choice of films included the *Strike in Dundee in 1911*, *St Kilda*, *Scenes from Balmoral in 1896* and the *Dundee Courier in 1911 and 1937*. Janet McBain's commentary had a piano accompaniment from Pat Cresswell and this proved a popular feature of the archive film nights.

The tenth anniversary of the opening of the Steps was marked by a special performance of *Madame Sousatzka* and an exhibition 'Dundee at the Pictures' which included a 35mm Gaumont cinema projector of 1911 vintage. Recordings of interviews with users of Grey Lodge were included. These recounted memories of cinema-going many years ago, some of them hilarious.

To encourage a younger audience, free films for children were a regular feature of school holidays. These proved so popular that staff had to put up a poster stating that "adults would be admitted only if accompanying a child."

But with the imminent opening of the two-screen cinema at Dundee Contemporary Arts, the Steps closed its doors on 20th December 1998 with *The Rocky Horror Picture Show*.

50. Gilfillan Hall - Whitehall Crescent

The earliest known date when films were shown at the Gilfillan Hall is 29th January 1897 when it put on a show of 'Animated Photographs'. Thereafter, it showed moving pictures on a regular basis, a typical example being on 15th October of the same year when it showed a 'Kinematograph Exhibition of Special New Local Scenes and Humorous Pictures".

Gilfillan Hall became a popular venue for the screening of moving pictures particularly when films were available of newsworthy events. In May 1901 large crowds were unable to get in to see a show that included films of *China and the Boer Wars*.

Nearly all the films shown in the early period were reality films such as news events or scenes of travel. But narrative films were being shown in 1905 as indicated by an advertisement in the Piper o' Dundee of 15th December which proclaimed that:-

THE NEW CENTURY ANIMATED PICTURES
are attracting large and delighted audiences to the
GILLFILLAN HALL
to witness their New and Brilliant Entertainment,
including the
Prince of Wales in India,
The Sailor's Wedding
Two Little Waifs
and 10,000 others.

In 1909, regular shows were being put on at the Gilfillan by J. J. Bennell under his B & B Pictures name. On 13th March, it was showing *Psyche* which it described as "one of the finest Coloured Pictures Ever Shown".

On 25th February 1910, the Gilfillan Hall was among the first venues licensed by the City Council under the provisions of the Cinematograph Act of 1909.

The side margin illustrations are of cardboard publicity handouts for a performance put on around 1914. A film of 4,000 feet would have run for about for 45 minutes.

The Gilfillan stopped showing films either during or just after the end of the First World War.

51. The Electric Theatre - William Street

Feather's portable booth in William Street, consisted of four collapsible wooden walls and canvas roof that had housed a carnival 'Hall of Mirrors' side-show. This was his first Electric Theatre' in which around the turn of the century he showed short, primitive movies.

There were three houses nightly at 7-8pm, 8-9pm (the most popular) and 9-10 pm. Seating was on wooden planks balanced on metal drums resting on an ash and sawdust covered earthen floor. Crawling in under the front staging to watch a movie for free was common practice among young Dundonians of that time. This, the first Electric Theatre, was sold to Robert Pennycook in 1908 who gave performances here until 1912.

One off Locations

In the early days of moving pictures, films were shown to paying audiences in a number of locations around the city - mostly local halls. Churches and organisations used individuals such as "Marvello", who in the Courier, offered to give "Magical and Musical Phonograph and Cinematograph Shows". These shows were often fund raisers and occurred for a brief period, when moving pictures were in their infancy.

The following are the dates and the locations where the screening of moving pictures has been identified (through the medium of advertisements) to have taken place. There are likely to have been others conducted on a more informal basis.

30th April 1897
St Mary's Hall, Forebank
Animated Photographs

22nd January 1898
Jamaica Street Hall
A1 Place to spend the evening
Tonight at 8pm, Exhibition of Animated Pictures
Bull fight, Hospital Procession Admission 2d

25th February 1898
Maxwelltown Hall
Animated Pictures and Magic Lantern Show
New Local Views – Esplanade Bathing
Admission 2d

20th March 1901
St John's Church Choir, Grand Concert and Cinematograph Exhibition to be held in Union Street at the **City Assembly Rooms.**

8th April 1901
Cinematograph Solos and Addresses
YWCA 33 Tay Street

3rd January 1903
Forester's Hall Ward Road
"Carnival Day at the Coalmine, Policeman's Dream, The Dog and the Pipe, The Mysterious Schoolmaster, The Glutton, The Match Seller, The Double Chain Mystery and Pantomime of Nursery Rhymes"
Living Pictures in Lifelike Colours.

Screen Credits

Although this book is primarily about the cinemas of Dundee, it seems wrong not to mention at least some of those Dundonians who were so taken with what they saw on the large screen that they decided to make a career in films and became actors, directors, producers or screen writers. Although many of these individuals also had extensive careers on stage, (and later in television), that part of their work has not been covered. The list of those Dundonians set out below is not by any means comprehensive, and contains no one who was involved with less than five pictures. It does however give a flavour of the range of people born in Dundee who went on to be involved in the making of moving pictures.

James C. May was born in Dundee on 8th April 1857. May appeared in eleven films, the first of which was as a taxi driver in *The Key* in 1934. His roles were always very small, and his last appearance was as a cockney in an air raid shelter in *Waterloo Bridge* (1940). He died in Los Angeles on 23rd August 1941.

Bobby Mack was born Robert McKirrick in Dundee on 7th November 1865. He made some 28 films in a career running from 1916 to 1929. His first role was in *The Girl of Lost Lake* (1916) in which he had a strong supporting role, and this was followed by a role in a cliffhanger serial *The Red Ace* (1917). His last appearance was in the 1929 drama, *Evangeline*. It would appear that he was one of the actors whose career did not survive the change from silent films to talkies. Bobby Mack died in New York on 2nd May 1949.

Henrietta Watson was born in Dundee on 11th March 1873. Her film career as an actress started in 1916. The film, a drama, was entitled *Driven*, and was directed by prolific English director Maurice Elvey. She appeared in seventeen films in all, every one of which was a British production. The last of these was the 1939 film *The Four Just Men*. Henrietta died in September 1964 in London.

Penrhyn Stanlaws was born in Dundee as Stanley Anderson on March 19th 1877. He later adopted Penrhyn Stanlaws as his professional name. Stanlaws started his career as an illustrator. Known as a painter of pretty women he worked for the American magazine, Saturday Evening Post, from 1913 to 1935 whilst also doing freelance work for other periodicals including the New Movie and Hearts international. Among his models were Mabel Normand, Olive Thomas and Anna Q Nilsson, all of whom later became successful film stars.

He built the Hotel des Artistes in New York where artists lived and worked; this still exists today. Despite his busy career as an illustrator he still managed to find the time to direct seven silent films in the years 1921 and 1922. Stanlaws died on 20th May 1957 in Los Angeles.

William Duncan was born in December 1879 in Nicoll's Lane, Lochee. In 1890 he moved with his family to the USA, living at first in New York where he became an actor. He got a job with the Selig Polyscope Company, a pioneering film making business founded in 1896.

Duncan's earliest recorded screen credit was in 1909 and he soon became a star of western films both acting and carrying out his own stunts. From 1911 he was also writing and directing. It is interesting to note that, around that time, Selig Polyscope had another Scottish actor temporarily on their books, as in 1914 Selig made fourteen short experimental talking films starring Harry Lauder.

Duncan soon became the leading western star of his time. It was no surprise then that, in 1915, he was picked up by the American Vitagraph Company. Vitagraph was at the time the most prolific film studio in the States. When he joined Vitagraph, his contract was worth $1 million a year, more than Douglas Fairbanks or Mary Pickford was paid at the time.

In 1917, Duncan directed and starred in *The Fighting Trail*, a highly successful western serial. This was to be the first of ten such pictures that made him tremendously popular and also very wealthy. In 1918 he co-starred with Edith Johnson in *A Fight for Millions*. She became his wife, and together they became a very popular on-screen pair. They made seven films together, after which they retired in 1924. At that point Duncan had made over 175 films in a career which successfully spanned the change from silent to talking pictures.

However, Duncan came out of retirement in 1935 - possibly a move necessitated by the effects of the 1929 financial crash. He went on to make another eleven films, the last of which was *The Texas Rangers Ride Again* (1940). After living another 20 years in retirement, William Duncan died in 1961.

Ewart Adamson was born in Dundee 23rd Ocober 1882. He went to sea at the age of 14 and later settled in Canada . He fought in the Canadian Army during WW1 and was promoted through the ranks from private to major while serving in France and Belgium. Supposedly he worked as a tin mine manager in Perak before he moved to California in the mid 1920s, and this formed the basis for one of his later film story lines. After settling in Hollywood, Adamson became a very prolific screenwriter.

His most productive periods were from 1926 to 1929, when he was involved with over 50 films, and the 1930s, during which decade he wrote stories and/or screenplays for over 65 films. During the 1930s he wrote screenplays for Buster Keaton, and provided both the story and the screenplay for The Walking Dead (1936) which starred Bela Lugosi and Boris Karloff. Although, in the 1940s, he wrote four features for Republic and others for PRC and Monogram, his work dried up after the end of the Second World War when demand declined for the short films in which he specialised. Over his career he worked on screenplays for 137 pictures. He died on 28th November 1945 in Hollywood.

David Keir was born David Keir Gracie on 7th February 1884. Initially entering the family glove business, he soon abandoned this for the stage, changing his name to avoid shaming his otherwise respectable family. As well as years spent in repertory theatre, he had small roles in over 80 films including A. J. Cronin adaptations *The Citadel and Hatter's Castle* and the classic Will Hay comedies *Where's that Fire?* and *The Ghost of St Michael's*. His later appearances included roles in *The Brothers* with fellow Dundonian Will Fyffe and Hitchcock's *Under Capricorn*.

Will Fyffe was born in a tenement at 36, Broughty Ferry Road, Dundee on 16th February 1885. His father was a ship's carpenter to trade but was interested in the theatre. He had a travelling Penny Gaff which he toured around Scotland. Will accompanied him and gathered experience as an entertainer which proved useful when, in his twenties, he joined a travelling theatre company based in Abergavenny in Wales.

Fyffe's first film role was in 1914 when he appeared as Lewis Bach in T*he Maid of Cefn Ydfa*, a drama set in Wales. This was the first of 23 films in which he was to appear but twenty years were to elapse before he appeared on screen again. This was his starring role in *Happy* (1934). In fact he starred in many of the films he made, and usually stole the show in any supporting role. During his time he starred alongside among others, Finlay Currie, Patricia Roc, John Gielgud, Douglas Fairbanks Junior and Margaret Lockwood. His last film was *The Brothers* (1947) which was released shortly before his death. This occurred on 14th December 1947 in Rusack's Hotel in St Andrews, Fife. Apparently, while recovering from surgery, he was overcome by dizziness and accidentally fell to his death from a window.

David Hay Petrie was born in Dundee on July 16th 1895. Hay Petrie went to the University of St Andrews, where he first discovered his talent for the stage. In 1915 he joined the Royal Scots as a Second Lieutenant. After the war he joined the Old Vic Company appearing as 'Starveling in *A Midsummer Night's Dream* in 1920. In 1924, Petrie went into variety with *The Looking Glass*, in which he sang "Oh Shakespeare you're the best of all but you can't fill the fourteen shilling stall". His first film part was in *Suspense* in 1930. Hay Petrie struggled with alcoholism, but was much loved by audiences and players

He appeared in some 86 films during the 1920s and 1930s. He was described as "a diminutive Scots character actor of quirky personality and the gift of the gab". Hay was always a supporting actor, apart from his role as Quilp in the 1934 production of *The Old Curiosity Shop*. He appeared in many roles, often as an eccentric character. He was noted for his appearance as the villainous Dr Fosco in *Crimes at the Dark House* (1940). This was a version of Wilkie Collins' novel, The Woman in White, in which Hay Petrie and David Keir (another Dundonian) played Tod Slaughter's partners in crime. In the last few years of his career he appeared in some of the greatest British films ever made, including *Great Expectations*, *The Red Shoes*, and *The Queen of Spades*. Hay Petrie died in July 1948 in London.

Ena Beaumont was born in Dundee but her date of birth although unknown was probably in the late 1890s. She made twenty two screen appearances, most of which were short films, and all of which were made in the United Kingdom. Her first role was as she first appeared on screen as Peggy Marsden in the 1918 production of *The Girl from Downing Street*. She later appeared as Mrs. Newlywed in *Everybody's Doing It* (1919) in 1920, she made a series of 6 shorts entitled *Our Girls and Their Physique*. In the following year she took the role of Tootsie Sloper in a series of six Ally Sloper films. Her last film was *Watching Eyes*, a drama made in 1921. It is not known where or when she died.

Evelyn Henry Mollison was born in Dundee on 21st February 1905. His career began just as silent films were giving way to talking films. In the period between 1928 and 1954, he appeared in 32 films. The first of his appearances was in *Balaclava* (1928) after which he rose rapidly through the ranking. In the late 1930s, he had a number of starring roles, notably in *Someday* (1935), in which he starred with Margaret Lockwood, and a crime drama, *Find the Witness* (1937).
When the Second World War broke out, he decided to return to Britain to join the forces. Unfortunately, the ship on which he was traveling was captured by Nazis and he spent five years in a German P.O.W. camp. During this period he organised camp entertainment and produced 56 shows for the other inmates.
On his release, he returned to Britain where he resumed his acting career. While he never fully recovered from his wartime experiences and only made a limited number of post war appearances, towards the end of his career he starred in

Chelsea Story (1951), a crime drama, and a comedy - *What the Butler Saw* - in 1950. His last film was *The Front Page* (1954) starring Jack Hawkins, Elizabeth Allen and Eva Bartok. He died in 1985 in Greenwich, London, in a home for actors who were down on their luck.

James McDonald was born in Dundee on May 19th in 1905. His family moved to the USA when he was only a small child and settled in Philadelphia where he was educated. In 1927, McDonald moved to Burbank in California, only a few miles away from Hollywood and home to a number of film studios including Warners and Walt Disney. After working for a short time as an engineer, he became a drummer in a band working on cruise ships. In between cruises he worked with local session bands. In 1934, he was called in to work with a band that was recording music for a short Mickey Mouse film at the Walt Disney Studio in Burbank. After the band left, Jimmy stayed on at Walt Disney and became head of their sound effects department. In 1947, he was selected by Walt Disney to take over from Disney as the voice of Mickey Mouse. He subsequently provided the voice of Mickey Mouse on all film and television projects until he retired in 1977.

He was also involved in many other Disney films, notably responsible for the whistling, yodelling, and sneezing for *Snow White and the Seven Dwarfs* (1937). One of his more bizarre contributions was to provide the humming for Kirk Douglas in *20,000 Leagues under the Sea* (1954). James McDonald died on 1st April 1991 at his home in Glendale, Los Angeles.

Ronald George Barclay Kinnoch was born in Dundee on July 10th 1910. He was a producer of films and a writer of screenplays. In 1936 he was employed by Incorporated Talking Films, a British company, as Associate Producer for a musical thriller entitled *Melody of my Heart*. He was involved with the making of sixteen films, including the classics *Village of the Damned* and *The Ipcress File*. His last film was *Inadmissible Evidence* in 1968. He died in Los Angeles on 22nd November 1995.

Harry Gordon Richardson was born in Dundee in December 1911. He appeared in ten films between 1961 and 1981, always playing small roles. He died in London in December 1994.

Sheila Shand Gibbs was born in 1930 in Dundee. Although her acting career was primarily in television she appeared in seven films between 1952 and 2001. The first of these was *Mr Denning Drives North* starring John Mills, and the last, a drama entitled *The Discovery of Heaven*.

Ewan Hooper was born in Dundee on 23rd October 1935 and studied at RADA. He had a long career in theatre film and television, his cinematic appearances including *How I Won the War*, *Dracula has risen from the Grave* and *Personal Services*.

Giles Walker was born in Dundee in 1946. He was a producer, a director and writer of screenplays. He moved to Canada and in 1975 began his film career by directing *Descent*, a short documentary. He continued directing short film and documentaries until 1985 when he went to the USA to direct the comedy *90 Days*. The last of his 14 films was the 1993 production of *Ordinary Magic*.

Brian Cox was born in Dundee on 1st June 1946. He started his acting career at the age of 14 at Dundee Repertory Theatre and trained at London Academy of Music and Dramatic Art. In 1965 he joined the Lyceum Company in Edinburgh before moving on to Birmingham Rep.

His first film appearance was in the role of *Trotsky* in the 1971 production of Nicholas and Alexander. Since then he has had a very successful and varied career on the stage and on television. His first starring role was as Hannibal Lector in *Manhunt* (1986) and he is particularly known for his roles in *Braveheart* (1995), *Rob Roy* (1995), and *The Bourne Supremacy* (2004). In addition to appearing in many major screen productions Cox has appeared in everything from serials to short films and documentaries, and has provided voices for animated films and video games, in countries all around the world. He is without doubt one of the most prolific of any of the screen stars to come from Dundee, appearing in over 80 films between 1971 and 2012.

Ron Donachie was born in Dundee on 26th April 1956. He studied at Madras College St Andrews and the University of Glasgow. After working in the navy for a year, he joined the 7:84 theatre company and later worked at the Citizen's Theatre for several years. Although his on-screen performances have mainly been on television, his film career so far has included roles in *Comfort and Joy*, *Heavenly Pursuits*, *Titanic* and *The Flying Scotsman*.

Heather Ripley was born in Dundee on 6th May 1959 and started her acting career by accident. At an early age she frequently attended Dundee Rep with her mother, who was employed there as a wardrobe mistress. During a production of Lesley Storm's play *Roar Like a Dove* one of the young cast members fell ill, and Heather took her place. A talent scout saw her performance and sent her details to various casting agents, one of which was casting for the film *Chitty Chitty Bang Bang* (1968). After shooting the film Heather lived in Ireland with her mother for a few years before returning to Dundee in the early 1970's where she completed her education. Later in life Heather became an anti-nuclear and environmental campaigner - which once saw her arrested outside the Faslane nuclear submarine base. Although Heather shied away from the film industry she does occasionally appear at *Chitty Chitty Bang Bang* reunions along with some of the original cast members.

Hamish Clark was born in Broughty Ferry on 26th July 1965. He was educated at local schools, Edinburgh University and the Royal Welsh College of Music & Drama before moving to London to pursuing his acting career.
As well as theatrical roles, his on-screen performances have mainly been on television and he is best known as Duncan McKay in the TV series *Monarch of the Glan*. However, his film career so far has included roles in *The Decoy Bride* (2011), *The Time Machine - Morlocks* (2011) and *Matha - Meet Frank, Daniel and Laurence* (1998).

Steven Brand was born in Dundee on 26th June 1969. During a period in his youth while spending nine years in East Africa, he saw films for the first time at a drive in cinema in Kenya. He returned to the UK where he worked in the theatre and television. In 1992 Steven played in the popular television series *The Darling Buds of May*. He then played a role in Beyond Bedlam (1994), which was his first appearance in a film. In 2002 he was invited to the USA to star in the fantasy adventure *The Scorpion King*. In all, he has featured in some 13 features and continues to work in film and television.

Dundee Cine Society

Quite apart from those Dundonians who worked in films, there were others who were so entranced with movies that they set out to make their own. The first cine club in Scotland was formed in 1931, following a meeting held in Bank Street on 25th February, it was decided to form Dundee Cine Society.

Early interest was taken in group production. By June the club's first 9.5mm film was well under way. This, *The Eaton Affair*, has long since vanished, but a 1932, production, *In and Around Dundee*, has been saved by a former member. Although the war caused a suspension of activities in 1939, meetings resumed in 1946. Later, the Amateur Cine World 'Ten Best' shows were first presented in **The Little Theatre** (where a board was set across the two back rows to hold the projection equipment) and later in Dundee **YMCA**.

A local entrepreneur, now sadly forgotten, was a member of the Cine Society. Mr J. Clifford Todd designed The Todd Tank and a 16mm to 8mm film splitter, both of which were sold throughout the world.

Some Dundee film enthusiasts set up their own little cinemas in spare rooms, sheds, garages, offices... anywhere that could be darkened and reasonably soundproofed. These would comprise separate projection boxes housing at least one film projector - 8mm, 16mm or even whopping big ex-cinema 35mm! Some enthusiasts would go the whole hog with neon signs, tip-up seats, atmospheric lighting, tabs (curtains) and masking for the various screen sizes.

These little cinemas were not money-making enterprises; otherwise they would have fallen foul of the professional cinema industry. In Dundee, Jim Brown had a comfy 4-seater, with the appropriately grand name, '**Brown's Playhouse'**, and Jimmy Smith's '**The New Electric Junction Picture Palace**' was a reception area by day and a cinema at night. Films were expensive to purchase, but friends swapped material such as old trailers and adverts to full-length features. Several of those early enterprises are still in existence today.

Postscript

As we wrote this book we began to understand that in the 20th century a special cinematic community was born, lived, worked and died in Dundee. It was this community that made it possible for Dundonians to go to the pictures. Some owned the cinemas, some worked in them. They were movie magnates, cinema managers, chief projectionists, second projectionists, third projectionists, electricians, spool boys, apprentices, ushers and usherettes, They worked in tiny cashiers boxes, in freezing or over heated projection rooms and in cafes. They selected films and they showed them.

Without this community, Dundee would have been a much poorer and duller place. Whilst the owners were known about and have been featured throughout this book, there was an army of people who provided entertainment for everyone but who were largely invisible and uncelebrated. During the writing we met some of these people, and heard of many more, but we know that these are but a fraction of those who were involved.

So we would like to give three cheers to those unsung people who brought happiness, excitement, fun and glamour into the lives of all Dundee's many moviegoers.

Lets hear it for Norman Barrie, Vic Bawol, Dave Bennett, Alex Braid, Jim Bremner, Jimmy Brown, Tam Butchart, Eric Clark, John Cobb, Bob Conon, Chic Coutts, Alec Couthill, George Dickson, Sid Drever, Bill Daillie, Davie Dingwall, Eddie Elder, Mary Findlay, Jimmy Forbes, Blair Forrester, Eddie George, Alan Goodall, Dave Gourlay, Jim Gourlay, Tam Gourlay, Alex Gowans, Martin Hill, Miss Humphries, Davis Johnstone Jim Kelly, Donald Kirkbride, Bill Knight, Jack Meland, Jim McTaggar, Charlie Milne, Lennie Mitchell Willie Page Jim Perrier, Roy Peters, Wiiliam Rae, Jean Ramsay, Alec Ray, Jim Ryan, Henry Skelly, Jim Smith, Jim Stark, Ray Stern, Mike Tyrie, Bob Wood, Alec Wright and for all the others who were part of it but whose names we do not know.

Acknowledgements

This book could not have been written without the active support of a wide range of organisations and individuals.

Chief among the organisations is D. C. Thomson Ltd and in particular Murray Thomson whose assistance has been invaluable, not just for making available the records of D. C .Thomson but also for his enthusiasm and advice. We would also like to thank individual members of D. C. Thomson staff, particularly Barbara Briggs, Susan Daly, Stuart Ross and Norman Watson. The staff of Dundee City Council were invariably helpful and creative with their assistance and none more so than Eileen Moran, Deidre Sweeney, Carol Smith and Maureen Reid of the Local History Section of the Central Library and Susan Gillan of the Caird Hall. Michael Smith of the Fairground Heritage Trust let me have amazing pictures of early travelling shows. Thanks also for the assistance of Gordon Barr, Bruce Peter and G. B. Millar for their assistance in locating photos of cinemas. Matthew Jarron's enthusiasm for film history and his helpful comments on the biographies of Dundonians in film were of great assistance.

Among the individuals, Norrie Robertson's help was invaluable, not only in making available previously unpublished material, but also for his enthusiastic assistance in locating members of the Pennycook family, of whom Jean Henderson and Norma Anderson were extremely helpful. Without the help of Charlie Milne it would simply not have been possible to write the section on J. B. Milne. In this connection We must also thank Donald Kirkbride for freely making available the results of his research on the life of J. B. Milne. This book has also benefited from the knowledge and photos of Alex Braid and Gordon Barr and the assistance of Doug Hamilton in connection with Hamilton's diorama. Ann Buist's contribution on the Steps Theatre was most helpful in filling in an important gap in the story, as was that of Alice Black in respect of Dundee Contemporary Arts. Thanks to Joyce Searle and Dick Gates for helping with the research, Liz Barrie for her help on the songs at children's cinema performances, Alec McLeish and Bob Gray for providing information and photos, Raymond Stern for giving an insight into working with J. B. Milne, Gill Paton for proof reading and Donald McDonald for the wonderful description of the King's Cinema on the back cover. Credit must also be given to Jimmy Smith, a cinema enthusiast 'weel kent' in Dundee, whose contribution of knowledge and humour was always both informative and fun.

Lastly, a special thanks to Jim Howie, a post card collector turned sleuth and researcher, who not only made available items from his precious collection but also actively sought out and found a number of important illustrations of Dundee cinemas.

Index

This book is primarily directed towards the history of cinemas and cinema-going in Dundee. For that reason it was decided only to include the names of film stars and the titles of films where these have a particular connection with the city. To aid those who are only interested in the cinemas the index has been divided into two sections, the first listing the references to the cinemas and the second including all other references.

Cinema Index

Dundee

Cinemas Outwith Dundee

General Index

Illustrations

We would like to thank all the film production and distribution companies and photographers whose publicity material and photographs appear in this book. We apologise in advance for any unintended omission and will be pleased to insert the appropriate acknowledgement in any subsequent edition of this book. In particular we would like to thank:- D C Thomson Ltd; ABC Cable International Broadcast, Inc: Artificial Eye: The Arts Council, London: BFI Stills, Posters & Designs: BetaFilm (KirchGroup) & RHI Entertainment, Inc: The Bettmann Archive: Alex Braid; Robert & Mylen Bresson/Argos Films, Paris: CTE & The Samuel Goldwyn Company: Central Office of Information: CinemaScope Posters: Brian Coe: Columbia Pictures Corporation: Horizon Pictures (GB) Ltd: Contemporary Films, London: Daiei Co. Ltd: ERA International HK Ltd: Dundee Postcard Club: International Centre for Photography: E.M.I. Films: Roy Export Company Establishment: The Fairground Heritage Trust: Filmverlag der Autoren GmbH: Les Grands Films Classiques, Paris: Robert Gray: First National Studio: Douglas Hamilton: Heydey Films: Jouror Productions: The Kobal Collection: Francois Lehr/Sipa Press: Lightstorm Entertainments: George Lucas: Lucasfilm Ltd. TM & © Lucasfilm Ltd (LFL): Lumière Pictures Limited: M.P.C.-CMF: MGM/UA Communications Co.: MGM-Pathé Communications Co.: Mafilm Pic: Mine M. Malthete-Melies: Mosfilm: MetroGoldwyn Mayer Ltd: Charles Milne: F. W. Mumau-Stiftung/Transit-Film: The Museum of Modern Art/Film Stills Archive, New York: ORF/Mafilm: Craig Muir: Bruce Peter: Norman Robertson: Paramount Pictures: Photo Cinematheque Francaise, Paris: Panoramic Films: Photofest: Pixar Animation Pictures Ltd: Radiotelevisione Italiana: The Rank Organisation Pic: R K O Radio Pictures: Entertainment Inc: Photo Agenzia Giornalistica Italia, Rome: Courtesy of the Romulus Collection, CTE (Carlton) Ltd: NMPFT/ Science & Society Picture Library: Seawell Films Services: Sound and Vision Corporation: Shochiku Co.: Edwin Smith: AB Studio: Svensk Filmindustri: Howard Turpning: Turner Entertainment Co. RKO Radio Pictures, Inc.: Twentieth Century Fox Film Corporation: Turner Entertainment: Universal City Studios Inc.: U.S. National Archives and Records Administration: United Artists Corporation: United Artists Company & Danjaq S.A.: Universal Pictures Ltd: Warner Bros Pictures: Walt Disney Pictures.